Shut the F Up and Listen

Matt Halloran

Shut the F Up and Listen

ISBN 9798990666900 (paperback)

Jacket illustration by Chafe Hensley
Book design by Anne and Chafe Hensley
of Weirder Wonderland

Printed by Ingram/Spark

"The word LISTEN contains the same letters as the word SILENT."

— Alfred Brendan

"When you're quiet, waiting for the next word, something incredible happens. You hear your greatness. Silence is where creativity lives."

— Matt Halloran

To my grandmother Gladys Halloran, who said,
"Matthew, you have two ears and one mouth,
so you should listen twice as much as you speak."

Of course, what I heard was,
"Shut up and listen more!"

But because she said it just the way she did,
her loving words changed my life.

Table of Contents

Preface

It takes a lot of strength and courage
to speak your truth.

Pick your example: Frida Kahlo, Oscar Wilde,
Rosa Parks, Martin Luther King, Jr., Tarana Burke,
Tank Man in Tiananmen Square.

Every one of them changed the world — because they
knew that in order to speak with such a resounding
voice, you first have to listen.

Widely, deeply, purposefully.

By turning their listening outward, they went from
simply being listeners to becoming engaged listeners,
and from being engaged listeners to becoming
the historical figures we revere.

That level of listening can take a lifetime to achieve.
And there's nothing saying you're a shoo-in for the
history books even if you eventually get there.

Still, my guess is that you picked up this book because
you want to make an impact and you're curious about

how becoming a better listener can improve your odds and get you there faster than if you were to try to take that journey on your own.

The question is: Has Matt Halloran written that book?

The short answer: No. Because the only way you become an expert in anything is to practice — and to keep practicing even after it's clear you're a pro.

That's a point Matt himself makes right at the start.

The slightly longer answer, though, is: Yeah, he kinda has. Because you can learn and grow faster when you work with a trusted mentor and coach.

This book is filled with stories that illustrate what Matt refers to as the 7 Types of Listening. Not only do you get introduced to key concepts like prompting and patterns of speech, but you also get real-world examples, along with exercises that'll help you become a more impactful listener.

Throughout the book, Matt shares personal anecdotes from his life and career as an ethicist, life and career coach, and expert interviewer that demonstrate how — and how not — to listen to build trust, earn respect, and demonstrate the emotional intelligence (EQ) the people you meet, talk to, and do business with expect.

As he says, one of the biggest obstacles standing in the way of our success is the fact that we don't listen well enough.

We may think we're listening. We may even think we're really good at listening. But most of the time we're just biding our time until we can take control of the conversation again.

The question Matt poses throughout this book changes everything: "What happens the moment you stop treating listening like a pause between talking?"

The answer?

Here's the coolest thing: Your answer's going to be different than mine. And Matt's. And everyone else's.

Because the aha moments you have while spending time with this book are going to be totally unique.

And, like Matt, I can't wait to hear what that looks and sounds like!

Derek Pollard, PhD
Safety Harbor, Florida

Foreward

April 15th, 1997.

This is the day I was first introduced to the man who would become my husband and life partner, Matthew Kyle Halloran.

I'd just started my new job at our local garden center. During my lunch break, I sat and tried to look friendly as the other employees trickled in and out. Some smiled and greeted me. As they did, I tried to match faces to the photos with names that'd been tacked up on the wall in the break room. My recall has always been pretty good — but I didn't recall seeing the guy with the shaved head and long, curly red beard, John Lennon spectacles, and a smile that instantly reminded me of Animal from The Muppets.

"Matt's in California on vacation," said my new boss, Andy, after seeing me looking at Matt's photo. "You'll like him."

The comment sounded simple enough. But it was also loaded, especially as the day wore on and I heard more of my new coworkers give variations on the theme:

"You'll like him. He's going to like you. You're going to get along."

I've never been shy, so when Matt got back from his trip, I walked up to him and said: "Everyone who works here seems to think we'd get along pretty well. So, give me your number."

I'm not really sure what he said in response, because my face was flushed — and (ironic, I know) I was hardly in a great position to be a good listener.

He smiled (and may have even laughed a little), grabbed a small scrap of paper from a desk nearby, wrote his number down, and handed it to me.

And we lived happily ever after...

Isn't it convenient how the story always ends there?

That's because what follows tends to get complicated. Two people coming together to figure out how to share almost every aspect of their lives without losing themselves isn't a fairy tale. It requires a lifetime of patience, self-reflection, and empathy.

Communication is often identified as the key to a strong relationship, but communication often gets equated with talking, when it's really listening that matters most.

At the time of this writing, one of the most interesting things happening on social media involves women posting and commenting about their decision not to enter into long-term relationships with men.

These women say they're tired of being mommy, therapist, personal chef, and maid to their partners. They're also tired of the emotional labor they're having to do for their families. They're tired of less pay, sexual harassment, not having autonomy over their own bodies, and the extra work society places on their shoulders.

So, they're opting out of long-term relationships with men in favor of domestic relationships with female friends.

The reaction?

Mostly anger, confusion, and contempt. From men.

The irony is that all these reactions are born out of ignorance and not knowing how to ask for something you want in a mature, respectful way. It's almost like what you see with toddlers. They know they need or want something. They just don't have the words to ask for it or the maturity to be patient. The resulting tantrum is really just an expression of their frustration.

Here's the thing, guys:
There's no need to throw a tantrum.

Instead, start listening so you can actually say what you mean in a way your partner can understand.

On social media, this latest femme movement has morphed into a hypothetical question:
Would you rather be alone in the woods with a bear or an unknown man?

Turns out, even knowing how dangerous wild bears can be, many women are opting for the bear.

Tells you a lot, doesn't it?

Matt and I have talked about this a lot, and it's led us to reminisce and reflect on our relationship, from that very first day at the garden center until now. What's the common denominator in our conversations — and in the stories you'll read in this book?

People only become their best selves once they start to listen. And you only really start to listen once you realize it's not something you've done well.

So read on. Learn how to listen to what other people are saying. Because that's how we begin to solve the world's problems.

Angela Halloran, MS
Portage, Michigan

You're
not listening

You're successful. You've got the CV and the track record to prove it.

But you haven't changed the world yet.

There's something standing in your way that you can't quite put your finger on.

What is it?

Like most people, you're not listening.

It seems like you're listening. But you're really just going through motions, waiting until you can talk again.

That means you're not hearing what the other person has to say. And that's an opportunity you're missing over and over again. Trust me, as someone who sees and hears this all the time as a professional interviewer, coach, and keynote speaker, this is where most of us fall down.

It's time to shut up and start listening.

Really listening. What we're going to call engaged listening. I use the word engaged because it echoes

ideas found in the teachings of the renowned Buddhist
monk Thích Nhất Hạnh, who taught Buddhism
as a practice that reaches out to the world instead
of standing apart from it.

This isn't a book about Buddhism. I want to be clear
about that so you don't feel like you bought one book
and just started reading a different one. But I do want
to give credit where credit is due, particularly
because we're talking about putting your listening
skills to use every day, which is one of the ways
Thích Nhất Hạnh taught engaged Buddhism.

What you'll find in the following pages is gleaned from
the more than 3,000 interviews I've conducted over
the past 20 years, as well as from my 10-year career
as one of the top 5 life coaches in the world (according
to *Success FastLane Magazine*).

Ironic, isn't it, that someone who gets paid to talk
is emphasizing the power of listening?

But that's the thing. It's not so much talking that leads
to change — because talking is about taking control
of the conversation.

It's listening.

And you can't truly listen if you're trying to control a conversation. You have to stop thinking of yourself as the focus while still being present. If you want to give someone your full attention, you have to set your ego aside so you know exactly when to stand back or step in.

If you're just going through the motions — what we'll call empty listening — then you're not learning anything. Certainly not anything of value about the person who's talking.

Which means you're missing out on all the incredible things they're sharing.

By the way, empty listening is what we've all been taught is socially acceptable:

"Hi. How are you?"

"I'm fine, thanks."

You hear the response, and you go about your day.

That doesn't mean moments like this are devoid

of meaning or that we're not saying anything
to one another.

It's just that these exchanges are superficial — and
for them to amount to anything more than a passing
courtesy, we've got to be particularly attuned to how
someone says "I'm fine, thanks."

This is where our work together begins. This book
will walk you through the key shifts in thinking that
will help you listen with greater purpose and intent
so you can lead while lifting others up and inspiring
positive change.

I want to be clear from the start, though: This isn't
going to be easy. Especially because we're used to the
loudest and brashest people getting all the attention
(which is why we often miss the mark when it comes
to defining influence and success).

But know that every success I've helped others achieve
in their lives and careers is the result of listening before
anything else.

So, as you take up the challenge of becoming an engaged
listener, I want to encourage you to keep in mind that

people pay attention to the people who pay attention to them.

And that's what makes people truly influential — they speak less and listen more.

Here's another thing you should know at the start: This book is going to be a little different. We're not just going to talk about listening. We're going to practice listening.

For one, this isn't a book of pie charts and bar graphs. I don't want to bore you with all that — even though my background is in psychology, and I could nerd out on those details all day long. What we're going to be exploring together isn't something that necessarily shows up in the stats, though.

It's the shift in mindset that's required for us to come together to change the world.

Each chapter is centered on a story or stories that illustrate the form of listening covered in that chapter. My goal in sharing these stories isn't to point out how unique they are. You'll have stories like these from your own life. I'm sharing them — many for the first time —

because I want you to become an engaged listener faster and more easily than I did.

With that in mind, you'll also see exercises at the end of each chapter meant to help you actually do the thing we've just been exploring together. These exercises don't tackle everything at once. They build on one another, just like the chapters do.

As a coach, I talk a lot about practice and, of course, the power of coaching. Let's take a look at a high-profile sport as an example. Professional basketball players have an entire pre-game routine. They practice dribbling, passing, and shooting. Do they really need to? No, they've done each of those things thousands of times. But they practice in order to warm up, get ready, and remind themselves of what they're about to do — perform at the very highest level.

They're also surrounded by an entire staff of coaches, all of whom help them stay focused and recognize the value of all the practice they're putting in.

For some reason, we as "normal" humans don't do this. We feel that because we've done whatever it is we're doing so many times, we don't need to warm up or practice. And we don't need to be coached. But we shouldn't forget that the athletes we look up to the most practice all the time — which is why we admire them as much as we do.

So, just like working with an athletic coach, we're going to work on specific things together in each chapter so that when it's game time for you, you have the tools and the intellectual muscle memory to perform at your best.

Ready to get started?

Let's practice

We're going to begin with something that seems easy but is actually quite hard. It's also at the center of everything we'll be doing in the book: Over the next several days, start to pay attention to how often you feel compelled to talk in a conversation. You don't need to track anything here at the start, but please be sure to reward yourself whenever you choose to stay quiet and listen — because those rewards are what build habits and change behavior.

The five types of communicators

We're just getting started, and you're already wondering what the secret is, aren't you?

Well, as you'll see throughout the book, the secret is — that there isn't one.

Everything we'll cover adds up to your becoming a more mindful and intentional listener.

Not much of a secret, is it?

But then, as I mentioned earlier, this isn't about shortcuts or quick fixes.

It's about developing the skills needed to listen so that when you speak it's not a matter of volume but value. That starts with knowing your audience, especially if your audience consists of only one other person.

In this chapter, we'll take a look at how you can listen to identify what type of communicator you're dealing with. Now, I'm not suggesting that everyone fits neatly into one of the following categories. But I am suggesting that keeping these categories in mind will help you become a stronger listener. And a more impactful communicator yourself.

Skydivers

Skydivers are people who jump out of airplanes but are terrified of anything with depth. They always have their packs at the ready and will bail at the slightest sign of turbulence.

They enjoy the thrill of the jump and often come across as daredevils.

But that's only to avoid sharing so they can protect themselves. You'll see them tuck into their dive the second you start to go beyond the usual small talk.

They'll get cagy and find ways not to answer.
That's if they don't just walk away.

Conversations with skydivers tend to go like this:

"Hey, how are you doing?"

"Great," they'll reply. "Everything's great.

Gotta go. See ya!"

Short and sweet, right?

I mean, it's civil enough. And it's not like skydivers are going to avoid you. They're just not going to open the door to conversations they can't steer.

Which isn't to knock skydivers, because on the flip side, there's no pretense. Their conversations are crystal clear and direct. Just don't expect any life-changing revelations when it comes to casual conversation.

You're going to have to listen harder and be a lot more patient to get to the point where they don't go into a dive right from the start.

Hang gliders

Hang gliders are people who glide through conversations. They're not in a rush. Although they're more even keeled and less abrupt than skydivers, they still avoid deep talk when they can.

Unlike skydivers, though, who tend to bail and not come back, hang gliders will ride the current back to you if you show interest. They're not afraid of more meaningful conversations. They're just not comfortable with them until they know you're willing to actually listen.

That's because hang gliders want to know they're being heard. They're used to people being empty listeners even when they want to go deeper.

So, if you show them you're an engaged listener, even in casual conversation, you're likely to stand out — and gain a new friend.

Here's how a conversation with a hang glider might go:

"How are you doing?"

They pause for a moment. "Things are OK." That might be followed by a sigh or another pause. "I mean, they're fine."

"Want to talk about it?"

They might look a little surprised because they're not used to anyone following up so earnestly.

"I'm OK, thanks."

This is often followed by a smile or some other small acknowledgment before they move on. But be ready. They're likely to resume the conversation later, as they know you're interested in hearing more.

Water skiers

Water skiers hold on for dear life. They're willing to brave the chop, but they know it'll hurt if they wipe out. Water skiers are willing to wade a little deeper into conversation right from the start, but when the waves start to pick up, you'll see them start to get more cautious and self-conscious.

Body language can often tell you when they've started to look for a safe place to bail. For instance, they might break eye contact, turn their body away, or even take a small step backward.

The key to persuading water skiers to stay in the conversation is to help them realize that falling down isn't going to hurt nearly as much as they think and that you're right there to help them get back up.

A great way to help water skiers feel more comfortable is a technique called reframing. Reframing is a way to change how someone feels about a conversation by showing them there's a different way to look at the situation.

You'll see reframing in action later in the book.
For now, I simply want to make the point that most
people are water skiers. I mean, think about it. Most
people you talk to are holding on pretty tightly,
going through life trying not to fall down and get hurt.
Conversations with water skiers often go like this:

"Hey, how are you doing?"

"Well, I just lost my job. And my relationship is ending.
Other than that? I'm OK."

"Want to talk about it?"

"Not really." And they leave it at that.

Wait, you're thinking, isn't that what a skydiver does?

Good eye!

You're totally right. It is a lot like talking with a skydiver —
with this one exception: A water skier will actually tell
you what's wrong (or what's right) before they move on.

Snorkelers

Snorkelers are people who know how to dive into a conversation while also understanding when to pause to come up for air. They invite deeper, more meaningful conversation, and they appreciate people who are willing to dive in right along with them.

Kind of like jazz.

Just like with the very best improvisation, you and the person you're talking to fall into a perfect rhythm, where everything you say compliments what the other person is thinking, and the ways you're communicating allow you both to feel seen and heard, almost like you're able to finish one another's sentences.

What do conversations with snorkelers sound like? A lot like this:

"Hey, how are you doing?

"I'm good. And you?"

(Note: This is one of the ways you know you're dealing with a snorkeler. They're looking to engage. Remember, the other types of listeners didn't ask about you. They answered your question, and that was it.)

"Doing well, thanks."

(This is a great response to gauge how deep your snorkeler is going to go, as it invites them to follow up with another comment or question.)

This type of back and forth is a clear sign that you're communicating with a snorkeler. And trust me, you want more of these people in your life. They care, they want to listen as much as you do, and they want to make sure you're heard, too.

Scuba divers

Scuba divers go deep and stay deep, almost like there's no such thing as "casual conversation." Most people aren't equipped to have conversations with scuba divers without preparing first. That's because scuba divers have done the thing most people spend their lives avoiding: They've gotten to know themselves — the good, the bad, and the ugly.

Rest assured, you're rarely going to come across a scuba

diver in the wild. But when you do, you'll notice it right away. They routinely say things that make you think, and they're not susceptible to the Jedi mind tricks so-called influencers use in place of real thought leadership.

To give you an example, I was interviewing this one really well-known PR guy. He had a genius-level IQ, and I thought for sure I was dealing with a scuba diver. But he kept saying the same thing over and over again. It was like he was stuck in a loop trying to drive his brand message home.

I was getting annoyed. But I took a deep breath (we'll come back to this technique in a later chapter), and I started listening even more closely to how he was saying things.

I focused on the four principal speech patterns: Pace, cadence, volume, and inflection — because when any of these patterns change, you're getting a clear signal to listen.

Scuba divers are likely to make these shifts consciously, which usually isn't the case for the other types of communicators.

A change in pace like speeding up or slowing down can mean the person wants to emphasize a point or really drive their message home. Keep in mind, though, that there are a lot of moving parts to consider when it comes to pacing, from cultural differences to varying geographic regions to individual style, so there are no hard and fast rules to follow. You're just going to have to pay particular attention to how the person is using pace in each case.

Cadence is the rhythm or beat of what's being said. When a person puts more or less space between words, that can also be a sign to pay closer attention. Cadence is often what draws you in and makes you remember what someone says. Think of the speeches of Dr. Martin Luther King Jr., for example.

Volume. Well, you know when a person gets louder, that generally means they're super excited or emotionally charged. When they get quiet, they might want to avoid your question, feel less confident in their response, or are testing to see whether you're really listening.

When a person changes their intonation or pitch, it usually means they're trying to get you to pay attention to something specific in their response.

People also change pitch when they've said something and you didn't seem to hear it. Pitch isn't something many people pay attention to — which is why it can be a listening superpower. Changing pitch is like highlighting text on a page or screen; the person speaking is trying to get you to hear something important you're missing. Scuba divers do this a lot.

OK, back to the story ...

At one point, I heard the slightest change in pitch in one of this guy's talking points and stepped in to ask him to ask about it.

He froze for a moment, then took a deep breath, smiled, and said, "You're actually listening to what I'm saying. I can't tell you how rare that is."

That was when the scuba diver dove deep.

It wouldn't have happened, though, if I'd done what the other interviewers had done: let all the incredible insights he had to share get lost in the salesy, one-way messaging he'd grown accustomed to using in his interviews.

Which brings us to a caveat about scuba divers: they'll try to take over the conversation.

So, be mindful about that and don't hesitate to remind them that they're not delivering a monologue. Remember, they're deep thinkers, so sometimes they get lost in their own thoughts. As an engaged listener, you'll know just when to ask the question that'll bring them back into the conversation.

Before we get to the exercises, I want to talk a little more about the importance of surrounding yourself with people who are going to support you in being your best self. I used the example of pro basketball players in the last chapter to talk about the advantages of practice. The other thing I want to mention is that those same athletes have coaches. Plural. They have strength coaches, shooting coaches, business coaches, public speaking coaches, head coaches, and assistant coaches.

What about you?

Do you have a coaching team in place to help propel you forward? I'm not talking about a single friend or your significant other — although they can and should be part of your team. I mean a group of trusted people with at least one coaching pro in it?

As much as I'd like to be that person for each of you, I can't be everywhere at once, which is why this book exists. I want you to have the confidence that comes from being coached so you can make all the little adjustments that lead to truly engaged listening — not the empty or casual listening most of us do our whole lives.

Let's practice

This chapter has two exercises. They both form part of your checklist for becoming an expert listener.

First, get familiar with each type of communicator we've just been talking about:

Skydivers — appear bold but will bail if there's anything deep about the conversation.

Hang gliders — glide through conversations always looking for smooth ins and outs.

Water skiers — hold on for dear life, at least until they know they can trust you, and then they loosen up a bit.

Snorkelers — eager to chat about life and their feelings, but know they need to come up for air regularly.

Scuba divers — dive deep, sometimes without any warning, and can push you to go deeper and deeper.

Think of this list as your personal scouting report, which you'll be able to draw on whenever you engage with someone, whether you've known them for years or have just been introduced. Knowing what type of communicator someone is is vital because communication isn't you playing against someone else, it's you playing with someone else. And that's what engaged listening is all about — being more mindful so you can communicate more persuasively.

Second, listen for the speech patterns we covered. When you're having a conversation, pay close attention to how the other person is talking. Are they speeding up or slowing down? Are they raising or lowering their pitch? What are they saying "between the lines"? Awareness is key here, too, because it's not just about knowing the players, It's about knowing the plays they're going to run.

Listening to learn

You don't become a deeply engaged listener if you're not dedicated to learning all the time. And we're not just talking about learning what other people know. We're talking about learning how they've learned what they know.

One of the best ways to do that? Listening to how they listen.

No surprise at this point — this isn't something you become an expert at overnight. It requires time, effort, and a willingness to reflect — even when reflecting means examining your own worst moments.

This is a huge step — because it means you're starting to pay attention so closely you can almost hear how other people think.

Story time

This is about a doctor I encountered when I was a biomedical ethics intern at a network of hospitals spanning eastern Nebraska and western Iowa. I know, biomedical ethics doesn't sound like a real thing, especially considering the state of the healthcare system in the US. But I actually studied ethics in college and have a degree in Applied Ethics from Lee Honors College at Western Michigan University.

I have to admit, there's something incredibly humbling about studying right and wrong. And then applying that to real-life situations, especially end-of-life decision-making.

My mentor, Robert, and I were tasked with conducting ethics workshops at hospitals. The nurses we worked with were almost always amazing. Empathetic and helpful, they'd show up with note pads, great questions, and a wealth of real-world dilemmas for us to consider and troubleshoot together. It was clear that they were there to learn, and I always looked forward to our sessions with them.

Doctors on the other hand? A surprising number of them were know-it-alls who simply didn't have time for anything other than hearing about their own earthshattering brilliance. Doctors like that would be considered sky divers: quick to jump into a conversation — and just as quick to bail the second it turns into anything more than a routine check-in or run-through of a patient's progress. To their credit, many of these same doctors came to recognize the value

of what we were doing after attending one
of our workshops — because they experienced
the power of listening to learn firsthand.

How it worked was that Robert and I would travel
to hospitals and lead workshops designed to prep care
teams for ethical conversations with patients and their
families involving end-of-life scenarios. Robert
was the guy who'd set up the internship I'd received.
He'd gotten the funding because he was so well
thought of by one of the area's leading MDs
and by the nun who ran the hospital system
(who turned out to be one of the most caring and
mindful people I've ever met; she made it her mission
to put compassion at the center of each hospital's
culture, even when dogma and other people's
arrogance got in the way).

On this occasion, Robert and I were teaching a session
entitled, "What to Do When a Patient Doesn't Want
to Do What You Recommend." We knew it was going
to be tough. But we also knew it would give us
a chance to get the doctors' full attention.

We began with a few basic definitions and then
moved on to a case study. The case study centered

on a patient who had terminal cancer. They'd gone through a number of treatments and surgeries but had reached the point where they didn't want "heroic measures" done anymore. (In case you're not familiar with the term, heroic measures means treatment meant to prolong a patient's life even if the treatment itself causes harm.)

Heroic measures are also a line in the sand for many doctors, who feel bound by the Hippocratic oath to prolong life at all costs. Unsurprisingly, the group of doctors we were working with that day didn't see any issue: The patient was wrong. And the doctors weren't shy about saying so.

In fact, they got louder and louder as we continued.

Here's a great example of keying on speech patterns. When the volume starts to increase like this, and then just keeps increasing, you've clearly touched a nerve, and that's something that needs to be addressed. How you address it is critical. Raise your voice in response, and you'll likely lose your audience. Lower your voice and slow your pace, though, and you've got a good chance of restoring order and having a meaningful conversation.

In this case, one of the doctors wound up shouting, "How can anyone be so stupid? They could have months or even years to live! There are only two reasons people make decisions like that — either they're cowards, or they're not smart enough to understand what we're telling them."

And just like that, we were at the critical juncture of the workshop.

Robert, who was at the front of the room, could have stayed where he was and simply brushed the comment off. What he did instead was brilliant. He paused briefly, then walked right over to the doctor, leaned in, and said, "Well, isn't that your problem then? If you can't convince a patient they should listen to your professional opinion, that's not a patient problem; that's a doctor problem. You're not communicating effectively."

At that point, it was like Robert and I were watching a cartoon where someone gets so mad steam shoots out of their ears or their head explodes.

"You're saying the patient knows best? That I'm not a good communicator?"

31

"That's exactly what I'm saying. And that's why we're
here. You see, there've been a lot of patients complaining
that the doctors at this hospital aren't listening to them
and aren't taking the time to explain their medical
opinions in a way they can understand."

Cue listening to learn.

You see, listening to learn doesn't just mean you're
open to learning. It means admitting to yourself that
even with all your education, experience, and expertise,
there'll always be something you don't know
or haven't encountered before and that sometimes
you need to hear someone else talk it out so you can
make your mind up for yourself.

If this doctor had listened from the start, he'd have
known we were going to share a controversial case
study that was likely to ruffle his feathers. Instead,
he tuned out — only to find himself becoming the
"here's what not to do" example in our session.

Which brings us to another key component of listening
to learn: Learning from others who are listening.
Let me say that again: A big part of listening to learn
is listening to others who are

learning while they're listening. It's an incredible opportunity to see how other people process information and solve problems. It's also an incredible opportunity to diversify your own way of thinking so you can scale your impact.

OK, back to the good doctor, who went on to say, "You're telling me I need to dumb down what I know? I'm a doctor. I'm the expert! The patient should have done their homework. Then, they would have understood exactly what I was saying to them!"

I chimed in at a lower volume and slower pace: "The person we're talking about did do their homework, and they made the decision they felt was right for them. Remember, Robert and I study right and wrong. Each patient's decision is personal. In cases like this, your role is to support the patient and help them understand their options. Not to judge them or impose your opinion on them."

"The only option in this case is to keep the patient alive!" the doctor bellowed. "Who knows, given time, they might even have been cured. But they gave up! All that tells me is that they were stupid. And weak."

Again, cue listening to learn.

One of the best things about workshops like this
is that you're connecting with an entire room full of people.
In this case, it was clear the other doctors had registered
what their colleague had just said. And Robert
and I could tell that they were shocked that he'd just
blurted out what so many of them had been thinking.
They were also realizing how crass and arrogant
he'd sounded.

That was the point at which the offending doctor
stormed out of the room, slamming the door as he left.
Everyone was just beginning to realize that they'd
had an experience that was going to change how they
practiced medicine, starting them down the path
to serving their patients with greater empathy
and understanding.

It was hardly the most comfortable experience,
and I certainly wish we could have had a more
constructive conversation, but as I said at the beginning
of the chapter, sometimes listening to learn means
we hold up our own faults so we can examine them
and change how we think and act.

And that's exactly what the handful of doctors who came up to us after the workshop said when they thanked us for giving them the shock they hadn't known they'd needed.

The other side of the coin: Being humble enough to know you don't know everything.

It's easy for us to point to the doctor in the previous story and say, "I'm glad I'm not like him."

Except you are. Or you have been at some point.

Because that's true for all of us.

Whenever we think we have all the angles covered, we stop listening. We certainly stop listening to learn. One of the best ways you can avoid making the same mistake the doctor made?

By being humble. Even if humility is often earned by inches, not yards.

Story Time

I was raised in a religious family. A very religious family. I was "born again" at 13 and immediately set my eyes on becoming an Episcopal priest. For many years, I was the lead acolyte at the church my family attended. Most Sundays, I'd help with two of the services.

Growing up, I asked a lot of questions. I was like a lot of other kids that way. The difference was that most of the answers I got from the grown-ups in my life pointed directly to God. "Why does the sky look like that?"

"It's because God is showing you His glory," would come the reply.

"Why are there rainbows?"

"Because God is reminding us of His promise to never flood the world again."

For much of my life, I took things on faith. I was content with answers like these, even though my curiosity never dulled. Once I started to learn about other religions and systems of belief, though,

I started to approach these questions with a newfound passion for analysis and rationality, determined to understand as much about the world as I could.

Still, I managed to miss a lot.

And I mean a lot.

Cut to decades later. I'm in my 40s. One evening, my wife, our two boys, and I were at home watching the movie *Thor*. Once the end credits started to roll, I asked why Thor was called the god of thunder when his superpower had to do with lightning?

Everyone else in the room, who had considered me kind of smart up until then, looked confused. Angela, who has degrees in Earth/Space and Biological Sciences and who's also a high school science teacher, asked, "Where do you think thunder comes from?"

Honestly, I hadn't thought about it in a while, even though we were living in an area that gets severe thunderstorms every spring and summer.

"It's when two rain clouds ram together," I said, feeling like the answer was as obvious as they come.

Suddenly, it was like I was in a movie, and this time
it was the scene where a group of people, a bunch
of extras with the three other stars mixed in,
were pointing and laughing at someone who'd
just done something really embarrassing.

And I was that person.

Thankfully, the laughter was good-natured. Still, it was
loud. And it went on for quite a while. Once everyone
had quieted down, I looked at Angela, only to see that
she'd turned pale as a ghost.

"Are you kidding me?" she asked.

I immediately started troubleshooting in my head,
trying to figure out how to recover. Should I play it
cool, like I'd been joking? Deflect her question with
a smart-ass answer?

Instead of panicking and making the situation worse
by trying to cover up the fact that I'd just given a wildly
un-grown-up answer to a grown-up question, I centered
myself in the moment and chose to own up to my ignorance.
I reframed my thinking. I reminded myself that engaged
listening often starts with admitting you don't know

everything — and that listening always gives you a chance to learn and grow.

"I'm not," I replied calmly. "But from how loud you were all laughing, I'd wager I'm wrong. Way wrong."

"How are you this old and don't know what thunder is?" one of my sons asked.

"The truth is there's a lot I don't know," I said, "and even more I've learned and forgotten over the years. Not to mention all the things I was taught that turned out to be wrong."

Angela leaned over and hugged me.

Then, she straightened up and, like the caring and compassionate teacher she is, she explained what causes thunder so that even someone like me could understand it.

I'm sure you already know this, but it turns out that thunder's the result of a burst of lightning. It happens after the lightning because sound travels slower than light. That's why you sometimes hear thunder without seeing any lightning.

My mind was totally blown.

And it was a great feeling, even with all the laughter at the start. Because now I knew something I hadn't known before. Or hadn't known properly. From that point on, I was always going to be able to answer the question correctly. Besides making me feel better, that'd mean I'd also (the pun's too good to resist here...) be able to enlighten anyone else who didn't know.

Sure, it stung when my own family laughed at me. But only until I realized they were just voicing their surprise. And in that short time, I realized they didn't mean anything judgy by their laughter. In fact, I saw that it was actually a gift. It allowed me to take a good look at myself — in the heat of the moment, no less — so that I could learn something I thought I'd known already.

Once you start to build that habit, that desire to keep learning and growing, then even when the process gets a little uncomfortable (or a lot uncomfortable), you're prepared and can listen past the laughter for the lesson.

There's nothing more empowering than saying "I don't know" when you actually don't know something. And there's no surer way to get the right answer or find the best solution than to open that door as wide as possible.

When you listen to learn, you lean into your humility. And when you lean into your humility, you're one step closer to where you aim to be. Because you're no longer trying to score a point or defend yourself or pretend to be something or someone you're not.

Let's practice

Here are another couple of exercises.

First, you're going to practice saying, "I don't know."

Yep, it's that simple. Well, kind of.

Even if you think you know something — like, you're more than 50% sure of the answer — let the other person you're talking to continue the conversation by saying, "I don't know." Ask them to explain more or expand on their thoughts.

"Isn't that kind of weird?" you may be thinking. "I mean, I know the answer, so what's the point?"

To which I'll respond by saying that "I don't know," followed by engaged listening is one of the quickest ways to build trust in any relationship. So it's a great skill to be able to draw on.

Let me explain.

When you're working with a client, "I don't know" becomes an opportunity to reinforce your expertise. I know. It sounds counterintuitive. But if we go a step further by adding, "And I'm excited to find the answer and get back to you," you've just reinforced your initiative, willingness to learn, and understanding that none of us knows everything.

In other words, you've shown how human you are. And human connection is only becoming more important in our virtual world.

For the second exercise, you'll pick a public place where you can sit with a friend. A cafe or restaurant would be a great choice, as you'll be able to listen without stepping over any boundaries between public and private. Be mindful of the fact that you're eavesdropping, and be as respectful and inconspicuous as possible. Start by listening to the conversations other people are having and choose one to focus on. Start with two people. As you begin to feel more confident, you can move on to larger groups.

As you listen, ask yourself these questions:

- What's the relationship between these two people?
- How long do you think they've known each other?
- Why are they here?
- What are they talking about?
- Do both of them seem interested in what's being discussed?
- Is one person dominating the conversation? If so, why do you think that?
- How far into their conversation do you think they are?
- If you listened until the conversation is over, how did it end?

Review your answers with your friend. What have you both learned, and how can you apply this to your own future conversations?

Listening
to hold space

One of the things that's become clear by now is that engaged listening doesn't just happen. It requires commitment and practice. One of the other things that's become clear is that when you do practice you can become a better listener. You can even become someone other people listen to to learn how to listen.

Before we go any further, let's take a moment to talk about practice, because practice is the key to change, and you're hearing me mention it a lot. So, what does practice look like when we ... well, put it into practice?

Here's an example: Mark your calendar, and every week revisit one of the exercises outlined in this book. Do that for at least seven weeks. The first thing you'll notice is which of the listening skills you've started to master and which still require more work. This will allow you to prioritize which exercises to revisit, letting you adjust your weekly calendar accordingly. Keep working on the exercises until they're second nature. Then test yourself once a quarter (or more frequently if you're up for it) by choosing an exercise and going through it step by step with your full attention. Note the ways your listening continues to grow and evolve as a result of all the time and effort you invest in it.

As for me, the long journey I took to become a more intentional listener is proof of that. Because, as you'll see in the following pages, I definitely didn't come to engaged listening fully formed. Like you, I've had to practice.

And practice. And practice.

In fact, I've had to practice every day since I first realized I wasn't always listening with my full attention.

So, how did it all start for me?

Story time

When I was seven, I was diagnosed with ADHD. That was followed in my late 30s by a diagnosis of depression. And then, at 40, anxiety. Yet, for as challenging as each of these diagnoses were, they also brought a sense of relief, because I could finally put a name to what I'd been struggling with and take steps to counteract it.

At the same time, adding this all up meant that paying attention was always going to be something I had to work at. And let me tell you, it's still really hard for me to sit still and listen — even after practicing engaged listening for as long as I have. I mean, even now, it's like a bird can chirp two miles away and I'll lose my train of thought!

So, when I say you have to practice listening every day, I'm not kidding. Especially if you've got repeating loops of negative thoughts playing in your head nearly all the time like I do.

How do you get better at listening when you're facing so many hurdles?

Well, one answer is: You do what you did when you first picked up a copy of this book. You seek out learning opportunities, coaching, and support from people you know you can trust.

You also take steps to start quieting your mind, which is key. You can't pay attention to anyone else if your own thoughts drown them out. Of course, you already know about meditation and prayer, how repeating something over and over can help you focus and create space for deeper, more reflective patterns of thought. These are both great places to start.

But I want to make it even simpler for you.

Just find a phrase you like — taglines work really well — and repeat it over and over until you can hear yourself thinking again.

My phrase? It's "I love you."

I can't tell you how many times a day I say those three words. I can tell you, though, that they help every single time I say them. And yes, I say them out loud.

This won't come as a surprise to any of you who know me as a speaker and podcast host, but hearing my own voice helps me concentrate. It also helps remind me that listening is really a love language. It shows others you care and sincerely want to connect with them.

You know this from all the practice you've been doing: You hear things differently now. That's because you've gotten familiar with the fact that people don't just talk using words. They're using their bodies, too. They're not just telling you how they feel and what they're thinking about. They're showing you.

Let's consider a few examples.

Look closely at their face, for instance. Observe their micro-expressions. Slight glances, quick frowns, and raised eyebrows can mean you're on to something or may need to back off.

Fidgeting is another great way to pick up on what someone is trying to say. Tapping, hand wringing, and nail or cuticle picking are all signs that there's more going on than what's being said.

The same is true for body positioning. If someone is squirming, turning toward you or away, or opening up their posture, they're signaling that words aren't enough to express what they mean.

That's a whole other level of communication. Tune into that, and you're hearing what the poet Walt Whitman called "the journeywork of the stars."

Which brings us to holding space.

You hold space for someone else in a conversation when you make room for them to share what they're thinking and feeling. One of the things you might notice when you do this regularly is that you start to visualize the space between you and the other person. "Wait, a second," you may be thinking. "Visualize the space. What do you mean?"

You've really gotten the hang of this, haven't you? That's another great question.

What I mean by visualizing the space is this: Once you really start to tune in to what the other person is saying, you're going to feel a connection develop. That's because you're not just going through the motions of listening anymore but are experiencing what they're telling you. This can lead you to picture in your mind's eye images that represent that connection — say, a tunnel, tollbooth, or boardwalk.

Or a bridge.

If you can keep those bridges open, you're going to hear the whole person talking. Which means you're not just going to catch what they're saying but how they're saying it. As we saw earlier, "I'm fine" can have any number of different meanings, from, "I'm fine, thanks," to "I feel like the sky's falling, and I don't know what to do."

If you're holding space for the person who's talking,

you're signaling to them that you're interested in more than empty listening. And this is true whether you're speaking in-person or online. It's just that when you're doing it online, you've got a little more imaginative work to do to put yourself in the same room and build those bridges.

You also need to hold space for yourself so you can experience the depth of your own thoughts and feelings and speak to engage, illuminate, and inquire instead of to react, provoke, and control.

To hold space for yourself, start with the same visualization, and then turn it inward. What does the space of your mind look like? How far does the bridge between your thoughts span?

I know, it all sounds pretty new age-y. But it can have a huge impact on your ability to listen. I know in my case it's helped me control my anxiety and de-escalate my stress. It can also help you get to know yourself, which, if you're anything like me, may be something else you need to work on through everyday practice.

Once you're able to hold space regularly, you'll be able to tell when other people are listening and whether they're actually hearing you. You'll start to register the meaning behind what's being said — the space between the notes, as the great jazz trumpeter Miles Davis described it. And you'll convey to others that they can say what's really on their mind without needing to be guarded or evasive.

You've heard me say it before, but I'm not sure we can hear it often enough: *Listening changes everything.*

Let's Practice

This exercise is all about examining the things we tend to scroll right past because they're so familiar — including some of the unconscious biases that interfere with our ability to be better, more engaged listeners.

Do you know about the Bechdel Test?

The Bechdel Test is a way to measure inclusivity. It mostly applies to movies (a subject I can't get enough of!), but you can apply it to any form of communication, which is what we'll be doing here.

The test includes three criteria:

1. At least two women are featured characters.
2. These women talk to each other.
3. They talk about something other than men.

Seems simple enough, right? But when you actually start to apply the test (which is what I'm recommending you do for this exercise), you'll realize how much work we still have to do to create a level playing field. You'll also find that you also want to share what you're learning about engaged listening with more and more people, because turning your listening outward is one of the most effective ways to bring about the change the Bechdel Test reveals.

After all, if your answer to the question "How many of the movies I've watched recently or panel discussions I've attended or podcasts I've listened to pass the test?" isn't most or all, then you've just highlighted why we need more engaged listeners. Because we live in a Bechdel world, a world that includes many different (often unheard) voices and perspectives. And what we hear, what we see, and what we say should reflect that.

Listening
to listen

The chapter title makes it seem self-evident, doesn't it? But after the first four chapters, I'm confident you know that nothing's as obvious as it seems. That's definitely true when it comes to listening to listen. Because we're not just talking about listening as a passive activity — you know, something you do while someone else is speaking. We're talking about listening as a creative act that makes space for the other person to be heard so that your conversation becomes a catalyst for change.

That's what listening to listen is. It means you become an empty vessel the other person knows they can fill with their thoughts and feelings without any fear of judgement or censure. It's not that you become invisible, per se. But it's probably as close as we can get outside of comic books, fairytales, TV shows, and movies. And, just as with the other types of engaged listening, it's so powerful (and challenging to do) because it hands all the power to the person entrusting you to listen.

Story time

At the time of this story, during the Persian Gulf War, I was enlisted in the U.S. Navy, and my shipmates and I were sailing through the Indian Ocean on the

ammunition resupply ship we'd been assigned to.
As frightening as that was (and just take a moment
to think about how you'd feel if you knew that you
were spending every waking moment living and working
on a resupply ship so loaded down with deadly
explosives that if the slightest thing went wrong,
you and everyone else you knew would be scattered
across a two-mile-wide blast radius), so much of what
I experienced during the quieter moments aboard
was so beautiful I'm not sure I can put it into words.

This was especially true at night, when it seemed like
there were so many stars you weren't sure there was
even any sky between them. It verged on the impossible.
Growing up in suburban Michigan, I'd never seen
anything like it. Even now, it's something I look back
on in wonder, in no small measure because all those
stars made me feel so much less alone.

On this particular night, the water was as smooth
as glass. It made it seem like we weren't even moving,
even though we were doing 20 knots. I was standing
watch. Actually, I was standing something called
"sounding and security." I had a logbook and a plumb
bob on a long metal line. At a glance, it looked like
a wonky tape measure.

My job was to go to different parts of the ship to make sure the ballast tanks were filled to the correct levels. Because if the tanks aren't filled properly, the ship can list and sink. It's a critical job. But it sucks — which is why newbies like me were the ones who got assigned to do it. To make matters worse, it was mid-watch, which runs from 11:45 pm to 3:45 am.

Because the work required almost no brain power, it gave me time to think — mostly about the fact that I was on a floating bomb. When I'd first come aboard, the chief boatswain's mate told me that if we ever took a direct hit from the enemy, the ship would explode and all of us would be scattered across an area two miles in diameter.

Needless to say, these weren't the most comforting thoughts to be thinking, no matter how ravishing the night sky was.

"Wait a second, Matt," you may be thinking. "Why were you in the Navy during the Gulf War? Shouldn't you have been in college instead?"

Let's rewind a bit.

Up until my junior year in high school, all I knew
I was good at were the things I did outside of class,
things like soccer, debate, dating, being a radio host
(if you can believe it, our high school actually had
a broadcast radio station!), and performing
in musical theater.

I had no idea where any of that would lead me.
So, when a Navy recruiter visited our school that year,
I was intrigued. (It didn't hurt that his presentation —
on nuclear physics, no less — was really interesting.)
I ended up talking to him for quite a while after class,
to the point where the next class was walking
in and taking their seats as he and I were wrapping up.
He gave me his card. Several days later, when I couldn't
stop replaying his presentation and our conversation
in my mind, I gave him a call. We went through
the usual small talk, as people do. I kept thinking about
his uniform, the confidence and quiet authority he
wielded, and everything he'd told me about the Navy.

I was sold before I'd even picked up the phone to dial.

Once I told him, he let me know that everything was
going to depend on how well I did on the ASVAB test.
Back then, this was the intelligence test given to anyone

who wanted to join the military.

"You score well," he said, "and the world's your oyster."
Then he paused. "You score poorly, and you join
the Marines."

He laughed.

I didn't get it. But I do now. And I'm really glad
I scored well! In fact, I scored so well I qualified
for something called the Nuclear Power Program.
I was going to become a nuclear power electrician.
It was a six-year enlistment. I didn't care about that,
though. I'd only spend the first two years in school,
and then I'd be on one of the most hightech ships
in the entire U.S. fleet.

The only wrinkle? I was still too young to get started.
I was only 17 at the time. I was going to have to wait
a year to enlist.

For my mother and stepfather, who'd seen me abandon
one interest after another over the years, the delay
seemed like another opportunity for me to move on
to something else. They were as supportive as they'd
ever been, but they were also understandably skeptical

about my stick-to-itiveness.

I was surprised they thought I'd abandon this decision, though, because I was super proud of carrying on a family tradition: My grandfather had served in the Korean War, my uncle had served in Vietnam, and my stepfather had served in the Army.

When I enrolled in the Delayed Entry Program, my mother was literally right by my side. She was the one who signed my contract, because I wasn't 18 yet. She never asked me if I was having second thoughts. She simply stepped up and signed the contract. Putting the pen down, she smiled and hugged me, and I shook the recruiter's hand. I'd just signed up to join the U.S. Navy.

That left me with my senior year of high school to complete. Even though I was convinced I'd made the right decision, I have to admit that it was hard to think about all my friends starting college classes in the fall when I'd be starting boot camp at Great Lakes Naval Training Center. Nevertheless, I took care of business, and we all graduated that spring. We spent the summer getting up to our usual tricks, along with a few new ones, and then I got ready to leave for Illinois.

The day I was leaving, my mom cried. (Just so you know, she's not a crier.) Then, during boot camp, I found out I was even more color blind than I'd thought. Not hard to forecast what comes next, right? I mean, a color blind nuclear electrician? So, I was taken out of the program and went into the Navy unrated.

Which is how I wound up standing watch on the night I'm writing about.

I was heading up to the forecastle of the ship (forecastle is the nautical term for "front"), and suddenly I heard shouting. It was midnight. Shouting was not something you were supposed to hear at that hour, and I was only armed with a plumb bob and a clipboard.

I cautiously started climbing the ladder near the ship's two mounted 50" guns (which, we'd all come to learn, were so inaccurate they were practically useless!). When I got on deck, I saw our security watchman, Jeff. He was pacing wildly, screaming into the night sky. I hid myself behind the nearest turret, not sure what was going on.

One thing you should know about security watch — it meant Jeff was carrying a gun. He was a Gunner's

Mate. His whole life aboard ship was about guns, from the 3' 50"s on the front to all the small arms we carried for security. He knew them better than anyone else.

In this case, he was carrying a .45. It'd been issued during the Korean War. But unlike the guns I was hiding behind, this one still worked. I know because I'd stood security watch, too.

Normally, the gun wasn't loaded, and we were required to keep it holstered. But Jeff had it drawn and was waving it wildly above his head. He was shouting so violently spit was flying from his mouth.

I could see his face reflected in the moonlight. He'd clearly been crying.

The next thing I knew, he'd loaded the gun. I hadn't seen him do it, though. Instead, I'd heard him do it — a click of metal on metal so distinct you'd recognize it even if you've never loaded a gun yourself.

And then everything went so still all I could hear was my own breathing.

The screaming stopped. So did the pacing.

"Jeff!" I shouted.

He immediately lowered the gun, wiping his eyes
and nose with his sleeve, trying to hide the fact
that he'd been crying.

"Dude, are you OK?"

"No," was all he said, and he said it in a way that let
me know he'd been wrestling a demon that had nearly
beaten him.

Not that I want to interrupt the story, but this does get
us back to speech patterns. I'd heard a little something
extra at the end of that no. It was a hesitation.
If I hadn't been paying such close attention, I would
have missed it. But that pause meant Jeff had more
to say.

I should have reported him to our superiors, but instead
I said, "Listen, I have 10 minutes before I have to report
to the bridge. Wanna talk?"

That one, simple prompt changed everything.

Jeff calmed down instantly. You could see it happen.

His shoulders, which had been up around his neck, lowered and his jaw unclenched. He unloaded the clip from the gun, made sure the barrel was empty, returned the chambered round to the clip, and holstered the .45.

Then, after taking a breath, he started talking. And he didn't stop for the next three hours while we completed our rounds. He checked the stuff he needed to check, and I did the same. I never once interrupted him or said more than a "yeah" or "me neither" so he knew I was still listening.

You see, my job — any engaged listener's job in a situation like that — was simply to be there for Jeff. To listen. And to hear what he was telling me.

It sounds so simple. But it can be one of the hardest things you can do. As for me, I didn't know it at the time (I hadn't become a student of engaged listening yet), but I'd become an empty vessel for Jeff. I had no agenda and nothing to say. I was just listening to listen.

And this brings up another important point.

Sometimes, in order to be the best listener you can be, you've got to break the rules. You see, Jeff and I weren't supposed to be together since we were both standing watch. But he needed me. And he trusted me to be there for him.

So, I chose to disobey orders — so Jeff could go on talking.

What he talked about isn't important here.

What is important is the lesson he and I learned that night: that there's nothing more powerful than listening so someone else can be vulnerable, honest, and real — with themselves most of all.

Listening, Jeff and I discovered, can literally save a person's life.

What's more, because of the bond we formed that night, Jeff and I have a friendship that's lasted to this day. That's something else I learned that night: Engaged listening requires you to take time. So, the next time you think, "I just don't have time for this," consider everything that might be lost if you rush along to whatever seems more important in the moment.

It's one thing to be a good listener. It's another thing to train to be a great one.

You've stuck with the book to this point, so you're clearly dedicated to becoming an engaged listener. You're not just counting the seconds until you can start talking anymore. Instead, you're showing people what the seven types of listening look like in action.

Because you're not trying to take control of every conversation, you're teaching while you learn — which means you've already come a long way. And it's with teaching and learning in mind that I'd like to share another story about listening to listen. This one begins in Estes Park, Colorado.

Story time

Have you been to Estes Park yet? If not, you've got to go. It's gorgeous. It's a small town located in a valley in the Rocky Mountains. It's 7,523 feet above sea level and is about 70 miles from Denver. If you go in the fall, the colors are simply stunning.

I was there in September, and not only was autumn
in full swing, but it was also elk mating season.
The elk in and around Estes Park are kind of talismanic,
especially during the fall, when they seem to own the
place. There's nowhere you can go where you won't hear
the mating calls that echo for miles off the mountains
surrounding the valley. And you definitely don't want
to get in a bull elk's way when they're rutting, as they've
been known to kill people who haven't given them
a wide enough berth.

During this trip, everything felt surreal — including
when I visited one of Estes Park's biggest claims to
fame: the Stanley Hotel, which was the hotel used as
the set for *The Shining*. It's super old and super beautiful,
but be forewarned: They play the movie on a loop 24
hours a day.

Needless to say, that doesn't lead to the most
calming thoughts!

I was in Estes Park to study with a guy named George
Kinder. He's the father of financial life planning.
As you know, I'm not a financial planner. But I was
building a program for a coaching and consulting
company in financial services. The owner of that company

knew at the time that the future of financial planning
involved more than finance, so he'd sent me out
to learn more from George.

For five days, we dove into every aspect of listening.
Not asset management or investing strategy, but listening.
We focused on how people feel about money — their
own money in particular. What were their hang-ups?
Why did they feel that way, and what did they really
want to achieve with the money they saved?

To give you a little additional context, I'd been
a practicing therapist for about 18 months. After grad-
uating from college on the heels of being honorably
discharged from the Navy, I'd opened a private practice
in the small town of Freemont, Nebraska. I specialized
in family therapy and working with adults with severe
and persistent mental illness. I realized I wasn't cut out
to be a therapist the day I came home from work with
tears in my eyes and my wife asked me, "How long can
you keep doing this?" (You'll see that this wasn't the
only time she'd ask me that question.)

While in Estes Park, I couldn't help but reflect on this
experience because I realized that one of the reasons
I hadn't made such a great therapist was that patients'

relationship to money rarely came up in the work we did, even when money was at the heart of the issues they were having.

During my work with George, we practiced his version of the "5-second rule." The idea is that whenever someone pauses during a conversation as if they've completed their thought, you take a breath and count to five as slowly as you can to give them a little extra time to consider whether they have something more to say.

That little pause changes the dynamic, in part because it makes listening more intentional. You actually have to do something in order to listen well. It also stops you from listening to talk, or worse yet, interrupting someone before they've finished their thought.

One of the things George pointed out was that when you give someone the space to talk, they're more likely to share. And that means you'll get to know them better and understand even more clearly what they expect from you and, if they're looking for help or advice, how you can provide it in a way they'll respond to positively.

We found that within 10 minutes of using this technique, the people in our group were sharing some of the most

intimate details of their lives. And that drew a bold
line under the fact that most people, when given
the chance, want to tell you a lot more than "I'm fine"
or "yeah, that sounds good" or "no, not really."

This is where knowing what type of communicator
you're dealing with becomes a big advantage. The technique
we're talking about here works really well with hang
gliders and water skiers, for example. With hang gliders,
you're giving them the chance to make their way back
to you since you've made it clear you're interested in
hearing more. With water skiers, they know there's
a safe place to bail out if necessary.

One of the other points George made was that because
we're emotional creatures with emotional intelligence,
or EQ, we have the keys to becoming an exceptional
listener. I'd learned this while training to become
a therapist, and it's certainly something I'm familiar
with in my own life (and not always because I've
been great at it). But it was good to get a reminder
that compassion and making an effort to understand
are integral to listening effectively.

What does this look like in practice? Whenever someone's
experiencing a strong emotion, for example, don't try

to redirect them or "fix" the situation. Let them experience the emotion, whether they're angry or frustrated or sad or overjoyed. If they're crying, let them cry. It's what they need to do. And it's what they need you to do — give them the space to be in the moment without feeling judged, controlled, or condescended to.

Of course, I'm not suggesting that there aren't scenarios in which a clear response is needed. Letting someone who's angry know you've heard everything they've said can quickly defuse the situation, for instance. But here, too, listening to listen is critical. Because if you don't hear what the other person is saying, you're not going to know how they're expecting you to respond.

Ironically, sometimes it's easier to do this with people you're just getting to know. It can be a lot harder when you're dealing with the people you're closest to. This was the first time I'd been away from Angela since we'd gotten married. On top of that, we had twin boys at home who were still super young. Thankfully, up until then, I hadn't needed to travel for work. But when you're a coach and consultant, that's part of the job.

So, here I was in Estes Park talking about things like being fully present to others, and I was nearly 500 miles from my family — and missing the heck out of them!

I made a point to call Angela every night. She's my person. And I'm glad to say that's as true now as it was then. We'd talk for 30 minutes or so after I'd wrapped up the last of my business for the day. Mostly, we'd just catch up and let one another know we were there for each other. And then I'd go to bed, wake up the next morning, and rejoin the group to dive deeper into how to put listening to listen into practice.

All told, the trip was a great experience. I learned a lot over the course of those five days and brought back a lot to share. But still, I missed home the whole time, and I was grateful to get back. I arrived at the house right after our kids had gone to bed. I went down to the bedroom they shared, kissed them on their heads without waking them up, and came back upstairs.

Angela and I went out back to the brick patio we'd put down together by hand and lit a fire in the fire pit we'd built. We pulled our two chairs closer together so we could enjoy the warmth and one another's company. I was excited to share what I'd learned, but I didn't want to do that simply by telling her. Instead, I wanted to show her what listening to listen looked like.

Plus, I really wanted to hear how she was doing and how her week had been.

So, I asked her.

Two hours went by. All in response to that one question. All I did was add a few prompts here and there to let Angela know I was listening, things like:

- "Tell me more."
- "Wow!"
- "Uh huh."
- "Oh really?"
- "Cool."

As I mentioned, with Jeff I wasn't conscious that this was a listening technique. But using prompts like these was one of the things George had focused on in his training.

Let me explain.

After you've paused for five seconds, you can add a prompt to let the person you're talking to know you're still engaged and want to hear more. The prompts should make it clear you're not trying to redirect the conversation but are just making room for the other person to continue.

In this case, Angela kept talking. She knew I was interested in hearing about everything she'd wanted to share that we hadn't had time for on our calls. I learned so much during those two hours — about how she was feeling about life, the boys, work, home, the neighbors, and our relationship. And, just like with Jeff earlier, time seemed to have disappeared.

When she was finally done sharing, it was pitch dark. And I was exhausted.

She noticed and said, "Let's head to bed."

As we walked into the house, she turned to me and said, "That was one of the best conversations we've ever had. What happened to you in Estes Park?"

I thought for a moment. And then I said, "I learned how to listen."

Let's Practice

This chapter's exercise is a two-parter.

First, you're simply going to shut up and listen. Yep, you're going to ask someone an open-ended question and let them respond. Give them as much time to answer as they want. (Best to practice this with someone you know well at the start so you can get comfortable with the process.)

It goes like this: Ask your question. Let the other person answer. When they pause or seem to have finished their thought, use the 5-second rule. Allow them to continue. Repeat the process until it's clear they've finished talking. At that point, the exercise is over, and a round of thanks is in order. If you're both up for it, debrief: Did the other person feel like you were really listening to them? Why did they feel that way?

Second, practice the prompts. Ask another open-ended question (e.g., "How are you doing?" or "What's one thing you'd change in your past and why?"). Then, if the person — it doesn't have to be the same the person from the other exercise — pauses for more than five seconds, use a prompt to re-engage them. Start with,

"Tell me a little more about that." Eventually, you'll use the full range of prompts — but this one is magic, so I'd recommend starting with it. Remember, prompts aren't meant to interrupt the flow of the conversation. That's why you need to use the 5-second rule before you use them. Otherwise, you risk coming off as just another empty listener.

As with the first part of the exercise, once the person's clearly finished speaking, thank them and ask them for feedback.

Listening
to build trust

Here's a question for you. It's one that's been percolating this whole time, so you should be able to answer it pretty quickly:

What's the common denominator in every meaningful relationship, whether we're talking business or your personal life?

Take your time. When you've got the answer, flip the page. If you're listening to the audiobook, keep listening after the pause.

That's right. It's trust.

Once you know you can trust someone, you don't always have to try to figure out if they're being sincere or just telling you what they think you want to hear. And you can say whatever you really mean without having to dance around the subject. This chapter, then, is about how to listen so that people know they can trust you. To show you what I mean, let's head back to Omaha. Before we do, though, I want to say that even though all these stories are intense, this one's especially tough. I mean, next level tough. Mostly because it involves a young boy who came into my life at a time when he had almost no trust left.

Story time

Once I realized biomedical ethics wasn't the career for me, Angela and I decided to apply to become Family Teachers at Boys Town. Angela, who was studying at the University of Nebraska at the time, had become friends with an attorney. She was a fellow student who was a guardian ad litem for a minor who lived at Boys Town. A guardian ad litem is a neutral person appointed by the courts to help make decisions in the best interest of the child. After she and Angela had hung about a bit, she mentioned we'd be perfect for the job. She introduced us to a set of Family Teachers. We all went out to dinner, and we came home convinced it was the right decision.

We went through an intensive interview process (which is exactly what you'd hope a charitable organization catering to at-risk youth would require) and were eventually told we'd been hired to join the Specialized Treatment Program (STP).

In case you don't know about Boys Town, it's one of the largest child and family care organizations in the United States. Since its founding in 1917, its mission has been to "save children and heal families." It was founded by Father Edward J. Flanagan, who was a leading reformer during the first half of the 20th century who "believed that children had the right to be valued, to have the basic necessities of life, and to be protected," and who "sought to close reformatories and other juvenile facilities where children were abused and literally held as prisoners."

That spirit still permeated the grounds of the Village, where we'd wind up living for the next five years while serving under the leadership of Father Valentine Peter. Because my wife and I didn't have children at the time, we were assigned to work with younger kids with much higher rates of behavior. Most of them were 13 and under.

What do I mean by "higher rates of behavior"? Here are a few examples:

- They'd throw things at your head.

- They'd tell you that your mother was a whore (although their language was a lot more descriptive than that).

- They'd scream for hours straight. (We had a boy, for instance, who threw a three-day tantrum simply because we told him he couldn't do something he already knew he wasn't allowed to do.)

And that's merely the tip of the iceberg. Needless to say, these were kids who needed a lot of love, care, support, and mentorship.

About six months into our time at the Village, we were called into a community meeting to talk about a new boy who was scheduled to arrive shortly. This was not one of our normal monthly community meetings. Fr. Peter (the Executive Director at the time) was there, as was Jim Daley, who was the PhD who'd created the entire cognitive behavior program. Multiple community directors were also in attendance.

We were all surprised when we walked in. Something big was about to happen because we never had meetings like this for only one boy.

As I've said, the kids we worked with were traumatized. They either had terrible parents, came from a terrible home environment, or were dealing with mental health issues. In some cases, it was a combination of all three.

But this new boy — he was in another category altogether. Child Protective Services (CPS) had found him locked in a broken-down refrigerator on his family's property in Louisiana. When they got the door open, they saw he'd been squatting in his own excrement.

He'd been locked up simply for refusing to spend all day working outside. Considering it had been summer at the time — dangerously humid, with temperatures well into the 90s — you could hardly blame him. Of course, the bitter irony was that he was even worse off in the makeshift prison his family had made for him.

We're talking about his own family here. Is it any wonder

that he felt like he couldn't trust anyone, grown-ups in particular? It's a miracle he hadn't died that day. And this had all happened to him when he was only eight.

When he arrived at Boys Town, he was assigned to live with our nearest neighbors. In our meeting, every Family Teacher had been tasked with a single, shared goal for this little guy: Start to rebuild trust by getting him to make eye contact with an adult — any adult. If and when we were able to do that, our next step was to get him to smile.

When Angela and I met him, we were shocked at how little affect he had. You could barely tell when he was speaking, and he didn't make eye contact with anyone. Even if you got on your knees so you were at eye level to talk to him, he'd look away.

He wasn't entirely silent, though. He would talk. But he'd only answer questions, even at the school on campus, and he'd also always end each sentence with "yes, sir" or " yes, ma'am."

Sidebar here. We've talked quite a bit about speech patterns like pace, volume, and cadence. It's important to remember that each listening situation and each speaker is unique. As we noted earlier, you want to keep in mind that different geographical regions and different cultures have different speech patterns. It's never the case that you can tell without first listening — and listening closely — what a particular speech pattern means in a given situation.

Let's take a look at volume in this case. Another thing you'd notice about this boy was his slow, Southern drawl. But you had to lean in to hear it. You literally had to get closer to him to hear what he was saying. He wasn't aware of it, but he was using volume to bring about the closeness and proximity he so desperately wanted but wasn't able to put into words.

OK, back to the story.

Our mandate was clear: None of us could take him out on any of our usual outings until he'd made eye contact with one of us. This was a cognitive behavioral program, which means it was built on rewards and consequences. Outings were often rewards, although sometimes they were designed as teaching opportunities so we could let the kids practice their social skills in real-world situations.

Achieving our goal was going to be even more challenging because we'd also learned that he'd been beaten at home whenever he'd made any eye contact with an adult. It was going to take us a long time to rebuild his trust.

But we knew we'd find a way, because that's what Boys Town was all about.

Turns out, baseball proved to be the key. Omaha hosts a huge, and I mean huge, baseball event every year — the College World Series. The event organizers always made a point of giving Boys Town enough tickets so that the kids in our care could experience a day out at the ballpark.

When this boy's Family Teacher asked him if he wanted to go, he replied with a soft, uninflected, "Yes, ma'am." She said, "All you have to do is look me in the eye and say that again."

Months had passed since he'd first arrived, and we'd all been working together since that first day to help him feel comfortable with this moment. Slowly, he looked up, tears in his eyes, and made eye contact, wincing as if he were about to get hit.

She replied, just as we'd been instructed to do, by saying that she was glad he'd looked at her and that she was never going to hit him for doing so.

Now that he'd overcome that major hurdle, he'd be able to join us for our day at the ballpark.

Boys Town had three vans going to the ballpark that day, ours and two others driven by two of the other male Family Teachers. The vans were those eight-person Chevys from the 90s. You remember those, right? Ours had a big brown stripe down the side and plenty of windows.

For anyone who's ever organized a day out with kids, you know that those trips can involve a lot of prep work. Imagine what we'd have to do to get this many kids ready! Besides organizing all the supplies we needed, we were also taught to do something called pre-teaching. We'd set expectations and talk about different scenarios that could happen while we were out. We'd do some role playing, all of which was designed to help the kids feel comfortable and in control on the trip.

On this occasion, we only had 12 boys and girls who could go. The other kids were either in trouble or had had something else come up that meant they weren't able to make it. Our little guy from Louisiana was one of ones who'd be joining us.

We loaded up the vans. When you're going on a trip like this, you want to make sure you have enough van space so that if you have to remove a child from the event for any reason you have a safe, familiar space for them to recover in. Having more than one van also meant we could take anyone back to Boys Town if we needed to without disrupting the excursion.

Everyone in Omaha knows the Boys Town vans. And we were always easy to spot because our outings consisted of a few Family Teachers shepherding as diverse a group of kids as you'd find anywhere in town to and from whatever event we were attending.

That familiarity made our trips easier, because the local community knew who we were and what these trips were about. And they were often incredibly helpful and supportive, although sometimes people would be judgy and actively distance themselves from us once we'd arrived. Before we went into the ballpark that day, we set some further expectations.

One was that we were going to leave during the 7th inning stretch. That was so we didn't have to navigate an entire stadium full of people making their way to the exits at the same time at the end of the game. To make up for missing the last two innings, though, we promised to stop somewhere near the ballpark so the kids could watch the post-game fireworks.

The crew at the ballpark always put on an amazing fireworks display — I mean, epic displays that rivaled anything you'd see in a big city on the Fourth of July. And this was going to be an even bigger deal because this was the College World Series.

Before the 7th inning, we made sure to get our fill of hot dogs, head-sized pretzels, and peanuts. We tried to keep the kids away from too much sugar, because, well, you know what sugar does to even the most well-behaved of kids.

So, there we were at the 7th inning stretch. The kids knew it was time to leave, as we'd been reinforcing that since we got to the ballpark. The Family Teachers began to gather everyone up. The kids all rose and got ready to leave.

Except one: Our little guy from the South.

His Family Teacher tried everything we'd been trained to do. But the boy remained non-compliant: No eye contact. No response whatsoever, either verbally or physically. I could tell his Family Teacher was tired after a long day of chaperoning. Surprisingly, the kids I'd been assigned to had been well-behaved throughout the entire day, so I was fresh as a result.

I told his Family Teacher I'd take care of him: "Leave me one van, and I'll get our little guy home safely." Everyone else left as planned. (Thankfully, this was just after we'd gotten cell phones, so I could stay in touch if I needed help.) That left me alone with an unmoving eight-year-old among a crowd that was already beginning to stir as we approached the final inning.

I gave it about 10 minutes. But our little guy wasn't moving. So, I started with the standard teaching skills we'd been taught.

No response.

Top of the 8th inning. Another basic request from the Boys Town repertoire.

No response.

I tried to turn up the teaching. Admittedly, Angela has always been a lot better at this than I am, but she'd stayed on campus to work with some of our other kids that day, so she wasn't there to take the lead.

I still wasn't getting anywhere.

Now, it was the top of the 9th. Six outs away from the remaining 20,000 fans streaming to the exits. Traffic was going to be bonkers, and I was afraid I was going to lose my ward in the crowd, as it wasn't like he was comfortable holding hands with anyone.

Then came the final pitch. The crowd went wild. And while they were cheering, I was nearly in tears, because I felt like I wasn't going to get this little guy home safely.

It was then that I leaned over to him and said calmly, "It's about to get really crazy in the ballpark. There are, like, 20,000 people who are going to be heading to their cars any minute now. I'm sorry, but we really need to go."

He looked around.

He hadn't been watching the game since the 7th inning. He'd been looking at his shoes. He suddenly noticed that there was a lot of commotion, and he started wriggling in his seat.

It was clear he was growing more and more anxious.

A few rows around us cleared out.

He stood up.

I told him what a good job he was doing.

Just then, the sky lit up.

He immediately grabbed my hand. His whole body tensed up. His eyes were fixed on the sky. Tears started streaming down his face.

Do you remember the first time you saw fireworks? Remember the awe you experienced? How scared, excited, overwhelmed, and amazed you were all at the same time? Amplify that by 100 — no, a 1,000 — and that's what this little guy was experiencing.

With every burst of light and sound, he'd squeeze my hand. Hard. Tears were still streaming down his face, but at the same time, he was smiling wider than I'd ever seen anyone smile. I was just as transfixed as he was. I mean, I've seen plenty of fireworks displays, but I'd never seen pure and utter joy like this before.

He looked up at me, locked eyes, and kept smiling.

He said, and I couldn't hear him for all the noise, but I could read his lips: "I've never seen fireworks before."

That was why he'd refused to get up and leave during the 7th inning. He'd been afraid we weren't going to keep our promise about the fireworks. And I realized in that moment that there would have been nothing I could have said or done to convince him otherwise, because too many grownups had lied to him for him to be able to trust like that yet.

We stayed until the show was over. He never once let go of my hand the whole time.

Usually, the kids sit in the back. But it was just him and me. So, I told him to join me up front. He looked at me and smiled again. I'm not sure either one of us could have explained what had happened in that moment, but it was clear that both our lives had changed.

For most of the evening, I'd relied on what many of us fall back on — our training. I'd tried everything I'd been taught, and as you saw, nothing worked, because nothing works in situations like this except giving trust the time and space it needs to happen — even if that's just the 30 minutes between the 7th inning stretch and the end of a fireworks display.

After that night, our little guy not only made an effort to seek me out and spend time with me, but he also started to trust the Family Teachers he was living with, then the other Family Teachers in our circle, then the teachers at the school.

That's the lifechanging effect engaged listening can have.

Let's Reflect

This exercise isn't about you going out and making someone trust you. Instead, it's about reflecting on situations like the one I've just shared that have happened in your life that didn't go as planned,

situations in which, knowing what you do now,
you could have reassured the other person know
you truly were there for them.

Before we get underway, I want to mention that there's
a reason why, provided you're able, I'll be encouraging
you to write longhand and follow the steps below in
order. When you write something on a piece of paper,
your body is physically registering what you're writing.
The sound of your pen or pencil scraping across the
page, the feeling of the paper, the smell of the ink or
lead — all of these things lead to what's called anchoring.

Anchoring is when you tie a sensory experience to
something you want to change.
This applies to so many different things. Practice it
here, and you'll start to see other areas of your life you
can apply it to — and other ways you can use anchoring
to build trust and become a more engaged listener.

OK, first up, grab a piece of paper. Title the page: Conversations that didn't build trust. Label the conversation you're thinking of, either with where it happened
or the person it happened with. Then, in all caps, write:
THIS IS IN THE PAST. I CAN'T CHANGE THE
PAST. BUT I CAN LEARN FROM IT.

Next, do the following:

- Make a list of what didn't go well in the conversation you're thinking about.

- In each case, take a moment to reflect on what you've learned so far in this book, then write down what you would have done differently to build trust as an engaged listener.

- Once you feel like you know how you'd handle the situation differently, tear the paper up into as many pieces as you can. Then, as you dispose of the scraps of paper, make a conscious effort to let go of the past.

That last step is really important, so, even if it seems a little new age-y, you'll want to do it. That's because this exercise isn't just about working toward a future goal. It's also about making peace with your past and using prior instances of empty or failed listening to grow into a better, more engaged listener. Tearing up the paper lets you close that particular chapter and move on.

Listening
to persuade

I've been in podcasting for a long time now. At the time
of this writing, I've conducted over 3,000 interviews.
More often than not, when I finish an interview, the
first thing the guest tells me is that it was a lot easier
than they'd thought it'd be and that they'd felt heard.

My goal as an interviewer is to help guests learn something new about themselves they didn't know prior
to our interview. When you lead by listening and give
someone else the opportunity to self-reflect and share
what they've learned, they wind up having a *very*
different experience than if you'd just shepherded
them through the standard Q&A.

Do you know Dr. Robert Cialdini's book *The Seven
Principles of Influence*? If you don't already have a copy,
I highly recommend picking one up. Although we're
not going to cover all seven principles here, I'd like to
focus on one of the them — the principle
of reciprocity.

Simply put, the principle of reciprocity states that
when you do something thoughtful and kind for someone
else, they're likely to do something thoughtful
and kind for you.

If you do something a little nice, you'll get a little back. If you do something really nice, you'll get something bigger back. It's how society works — well, it's how society should work. I know some people take and take and never give back. Like me, you'll encounter plenty of those people in your life and career, and you need to leave those relationships as quickly as you can. They're toxic, even over the short term.

Instead, look to surround yourself with people who're willing and eager to give back. They're the ones who are going to lift you up so you can lift others up in turn. Call it whatever you'd like — karma, doing good deeds, or whatever you're comfortable with. The important thing is that reciprocity works, and getting on the good side of the give-and-take we face every day pays serious dividends.

This brings us to one of the things we haven't really talked about until now, although I know it's been on your mind: The choice you make as an engaged listener. The truth is that you're unlocking an incredibly powerful tool. Are you going to use listening for the greater good or simply to enrich yourself?

You know what my decision has been, because this entire

book is about being fully present to others, which I believe makes the world a better place. And that stems from having watched my mom practice engaged listening throughout my childhood and teenage years. My mom's an amazing listener who built a career for herself by holding space for others and earning their trust and respect.

Before we take a look at how my mother impacted the people around her, though, I want to share a story about someone who used the power of listening for their own personal gain — without giving a sh%* about anyone else. It just so happens I know this other person as well as I know my mom.

That's because he's my father.

Story time

My father wasn't in my life much after I turned seven. He came and went as many fathers tended to do after divorce at that time. So, it was only as I got older that I learned more about him. One of the things I learned was that he was equally responsible for my listening abilities.

Unlike my mother, though, he could make you feel like you were the most important person in the world within minutes — without meaning any of it. How did he manage to build trust in a fraction of the time it would take my mother? He used compliments and appeared to hang on your every word, as if you were delivering the most spectacular TED Talk ever.

But in my dad's case, it was all a ruse. He only did this when he wanted something from you. And he was such a skilled listener that you would have already given him whatever he wanted before you even realized you'd said yes. He practiced every aspect of engaged listening, which means he was able to pinpoint what type of listener you were within seconds and learn what you were saying "between the lines" with your speech patterns and body language — all of which he could turn to his advantage in the blink of an eye.

I didn't realize my father did this until I saw the same behavior creep into my own life. Thankfully, by that time, I had at least some inkling that you could use the power of listening for good just as easily as you could for taking advantage of others.

So, what did my father do that went against everything

we've been exploring in this book? He fleeced people out of their money. That's right, he was a con man.

He was caught embezzling at work, and he stole money from his own family. In every case, he'd turned on the charm, feigning interest and concern when all he was after was making a quick buck and moving on before anyone was the wiser.

Besides breaking the law, he'd also manipulate people just to see how far he could maneuver them without their realizing what he was doing. When I was about 10, my father took my older brother and me out to a restaurant, to spoil us, as usual. He had his customary wad of cash with him, and he was flashing it every chance he got. (I'm still amazed he never got robbed!)

The waitress came over. She wasn't wearing a name tag, so he asked her name. It was Marie. Even then, as young and inexperienced as I was, I knew that once he learned her name he was going to start toying with her, seeing what he could get her to do, showing my brother and me how powerful he was. He'd done it often enough we were used to it. "Tell me about yourself," he said. He stared directly into her eyes with a gentle but inter-ested expression. His whole face softened.

Next, he'd "let them talk," as he put it, as long as they could or, if they were at work like Marie, as long as they were allowed to. Most of the time, the waitress would catch herself after a few minutes and would excuse herself to help other guests.

After she'd left, my father would look at my brother and me and say, "Watch when she comes back. No one ever asks waitresses about themselves."

The waitress would almost always come back to our table as quickly as she could, feeling like my father really cared about who she was and what they were talking about. This is when he'd take control of the conversation. He knew he'd listened enough to make the waitress feel special and that he could now turn whatever screws he wanted.

He'd immediately order off the menu, making the waitress feel important for being able to get the kitchen to make something special. He'd say things like, "I've run restaurants like this before, and I know you can get the kitchen to do anything you want. Cooks love to be challenged, right?"

He wouldn't wait for a response. He knew better than

that. He'd just keep going. He'd also bring my brother and me into the conversation to make the waitress feel like she was even more special for helping his kids, too.

He'd get upset if she couldn't do it. He wouldn't yell or make a scene. He was much cleverer than that. He'd simply change his expression and intonation to register disappointment. The waitress couldn't help but notice, and my father's frustration would weigh on her, making her feel guilty and suddenly less important.

If the waitress could do what he asked, he'd shower her with praise and ask her even more questions. He'd always remember key points from her previous responses and add them in to follow up or make a new request. And that's with his own kids sitting at the table! Can you imagine how many more times he did this? And how many other people he hurt in the process?

That said, I'm grateful for these early lessons because they showed me what a powerful tool listening can be. I had to do a lot of heavy lifting on my own to go from that awareness to using listening for good, because my father was showing me just the opposite whenever he was around. But in the end, his bad example paved the way for me to become the type of engaged listener who understands that our own success isn't determined by our hustle and guile but by how much success we help others achieve.

And that brings us to my mother, Jean. The first time I saw my mom exercise her superpower was when she was at one of the two nonprofits she led. At the time, she was the executive director for both the Red Cross and the Hospital Hospitality House in Kalamazoo.

The Hospital Hospitality House is a place, kind of like the Ronald McDonald House, where you can stay when a loved one is in the hospital and you don't have the money to stay in a hotel. Many of my mom's guests were dealing with end-of-life issues with family members in the hospital. My mom would sit with them for hours, listening to stories about their loved ones, crying along with them, hugging them, and making them feel as if their family members were the most important people she knew. Unlike my father, though, she meant every word and gesture.

Do you see the power in this? It wasn't just that my mom made people feel better in the moment. By reassuring them that they were being seen and heard, she made them feel better about a future that still seemed terribly uncertain. She gave them the peace they needed to bring peace to their family members and themselves. She fueled their strength and courage by listening without reservation or judgement and by nurturing them.

What's amazing is that these people who couldn't afford to stay in a hotel would often come back with donations to fund the Hospital Hospitality House. They'd write notes and share them with the team, letting them know that this place had felt like the home they'd needed during their loved one's hospitalization.

My mother chose to use listening for good by recognizing the power she wielded and not turning it against people for her own personal and professional gain. In doing so, she highlighted how much more powerful she was than my father, and she taught me, long before I realized it, the principle of reciprocity.

She also taught me that listening is a kindness, and that practicing kindness is one of the boldest, most impactful, and rewarding actions you can take.

Let's Practice

Here's another reflection-based exercise.

Look back on a situation in your life when you became aware that listening had given you power over someone else:

- How did you choose to wield that power?

- How did your decision make you feel?

- What was the outcome of your interaction with the person in question?

- What would you do differently now that you're on the path to becoming a reciprocal listener?

Based on your reflection and everything you're learning in this book, and thinking about Dr. Cialdini's principle of reciprocity, how do you see yourself putting engaged listening into practice? Who do you know who would benefit from it?

Listening to amplify others

Stories are at the core of human experience. So much so that we keep developing technologies to make listening to and telling stories as easy as possible no matter where you are in the world. We've even made a habit of sending our stories to the farthest corners of the galaxy in the hope that there's someone out there to hear them.

As for me? I've been fortunate to be at the center of the podcast revolution. That's allowed me to share the stories of thousands of guests and fellow podcast hosts. The coolest part is that it never gets old. Even an otherwise dry interview comes to life the moment someone opens up about what gets them out of bed in the morning or sets their teeth on edge.

That doesn't always happen naturally, though. That's where engaged listening becomes a superpower. You can hear it at work in every one of your favorite interviews: The interviewer knows exactly when to step in and prompt the other person so you don't just hear another Q&A but a conversation so authentic it doesn't even seem like an interview.

Just as importantly, the interviewer knows when to step out of the way so that their guest can continue a riveting story or carry on beyond their talking points.

They'll use all the skills we've been exploring, from identifying what kind of communicator their guest is to using techniques like reframing and the 5-second rule.

This book wouldn't exist if I hadn't spent years honing my craft as an interviewer by testing everything I'm sharing with you. Nor would it exist if I hadn't kept studying my heroes and mentors at work. One of the most important things they taught me? That even when they say otherwise at the start, people love to be interviewed.

Sure, not everyone loves to be recorded. In fact, some people will do everything they can to avoid it. At least at the start. But we all love to tell our stories. And when an interviewer knows this, you can tell, because they go into every interview looking for ways to hold space for their guests so they feel comfortable sharing the stories they're most passionate about.

As I've mentioned before, I wasn't always a great listener. Same goes for being an interviewer and podcast host. Just like you, I had to start somewhere and practice. And practice. And practice. On top of that, I knew I needed to pay extra close attention to the interviewers

I admired and followed closely.

Here are a few of the people who influenced me the most, along with some of the lessons I learned from them.

Keep in mind these are my idols, and that you may not hold them in the same high regard. That's perfectly fine, because the lessons they have to teach aren't limited to our evaluations of them as people. I know it can be a fine line, separating the artist (or the interviewer) from their work, but I'd like to encourage you to do so in this case, as you can learn so much about engaged listening from the following people.

Phil Donahue:
Using the power of silence

When I was growing up, daytime television was a really big deal. It was full of talk shows, game shows, and soap operas. One day during my senior year of high school, I was home sick from school (or was playing hooky, I can't quite remember which). I was watching *The Price Is Right*. I was hoping to fall back to sleep

but couldn't quite manage, which meant that once
the show was over I started watching the next one.
It just so happened that the next one was *Donahue*,
hosted by this bespectacled, silverhaired
guy named Phil Donahue.

I didn't know it at the time, but *Donahue* was *the* daytime talk show, and all the most famous (and some of
the most infamous) people at the time appeared on it.

One of the things I noticed at the time, which is almost
always one of the things comedians doing Donahue
impersonations focus on, was his use of silence.
I was so captivated by what I saw that day that I started
watching Donahue during school holidays and summer
vacation — and whenever else I happened to be home
from school during the day.

The interview I come back to even now is the two-
parter in 1990 in which Donahue interviewed Louis
Farrakhan, the controversial leader of the Nation of
Islam. At the time, many interviewers and audiences,
challenged by Farrakhan's views, wouldn't allow him
to speak without interrupting him and talking over
him, sometimes even shouting him down.

Donahue, on the other hand, gave him the space to speak without interruption and ensured that the studio audience did the same. His stepping out of the way like that was nothing short of extraordinary. It would have been easy for him to challenge Farrakhan like so many other interviewers have done over the course of his life and career. Instead, he showed an incredible trust in his viewers and listeners, allowing them to hear what Farrakhan was saying so they could form their own opinion about the man and his mission.

As many of you know, "dead air" on TV, radio, or podcasts is considered a major mistake. Donahue showed us over and over again how wrong we can be about that, strategically using silence to allow his guests to reflect and be mindful instead of just answering one question after another rapid-fire.

Donahue would let his guest finish their point, the studio camera would pan to him, he'd hold up his mic as if he were about to ask a follow up question — and then he'd lower the mic, giving the guest time to collect their thoughts and take the conversation even deeper.

He did the same thing with Farrakhan. He let him go on for what turned into a two-part interview. If you haven't seen it or it's been a minute, I encourage you to do a search on YouTube or the web. It's definitely worth watching, even if you find Farrakhan's views unpalatable. Focus on Donahue. Note how he conducts the interview without getting in Farrakhan's way.

This is just one of the many lessons Donahue taught us: You earn your audience's respect when you show restraint and integrity during even the most challenging interviews. When you get heated, it can be hard to keep your cool. Watch how Donahue does it, and practice putting that same discipline into action.

Don't speed up the 5-second rule, for example. And in those cases when you know you're about to say something right before the other person continues, close your mouth and let them finish. This is something I remind myself to do all the time, both in podcasting and my personal life. That's because it's so effective, and I thank Donahue for highlighting it so eloquently throughout his career.

Oprah Winfrey: Holding space

You may not have known about Phil Donahue before picking up this book, but I can all but guarantee you know who Oprah Winfrey is.

You may not have followed her early career as a TV news anchor, but you're probably familiar with her extraordinarily popular talk show, production studio, and OWN Network. I'm not sure there's much more to be said about the level of Oprah's success.
Her accomplishments and awards speak for themselves.

But I do want to take a look at one of her many super-powers: Her ability to make her talk show guests so comfortable they'd forget they were being interviewed in front of a live studio audience and millions of TV viewers. When you go back and watch episodes of *The Oprah Winfrey Show*, you'll see (or perhaps you already remember) the countless times a guest would unexpectedly cry or say something they'd never said in public before.

How did Oprah do it?

First, she listened with her full attention. Just like Donahue, you can actually see her doing this during interviews. Second, she held space for the person being interviewed — and when she did, she created a mirror, as well as a bridge, that let them know how closely she was paying attention.

Watch Oprah's body language to see what I mean. It's like everything else in the TV studio falls away, and all that's left is Oprah and her guest and the conversation they're having.

Her interview with Whitney Houston is a great example. Houston admitted after the interview that she'd shared things she'd never spoken of in public before. Oprah laid the groundwork by first creating a safe, supportive environment. Then, she held space for Houston by creating a physical mirror that blurred everything other than the two of them and their conversation.

What Oprah did — and what she continues to do so exceptionally well — wasn't a pantomime. It's much subtler than that (and this is what I mean by creating a mirror for her guest); She'd lean back when her guest leaned back, uncross her legs shortly after they did. These "quiet" actions served to reinforce the deep listening she was doing, even if her guest only registered them unconsciously. She was showing them that she was listening with her whole body — and that what they had to say really mattered.

Even now, when Oprah leans in during one of her interviews, that's the point at which you know the rest of the room has just faded into the background for her guest and   that whatever follows is going to be earnest and unfiltered.

This is another one of the ways you can communicate without saying anything. It's also another way you can build trust with whomever you're talking to. Use your whole body to listen. Hold space for them by building a bridge and holding up a mirror.

Terry Gross: Showing up without showing off

Now we're going to explore what I call the Terry Gross Effect.

You know Terry Gross, right? The host of the long-running NPR show *Fresh Air*? If not, time to put down the book and listen to an episode or two. Or three. Or four.

Considering Fresh Air's been on the air since 1975, you've got a lot of interviews to choose from!

Why do I call this the Terry Gross Effect? Because Gross has made a career out of preparing for interviews with people who've spent their careers giving them. That means she's almost always dealing with guests who've been asked every question under the sun, particularly about their latest project and the highlights (and lowlights) of their career.

Two things Gross does exceptionally well — and you'll hear her do this over and over again — are:

- Ask permission to move on to harder, more revealing questions.
- Give listeners context without upstaging her guests.

She blends journalistic rigor with an enthusiast's passion for learning and discovery. And she's never afraid to wade deeper into a conversation.

I remember one interview where Gross brought up the

times she'd previously interviewed Prince. She didn't bring Prince into the conversation simply to name-drop him or show off her own credentials. She did it to highlight her guest's talent and experience. She knew that by mentioning Prince she'd draw a parallel for her listeners, a parallel they'd recognize instantly and could then explore further on their own. She also knew that it would give her guest an opportunity to talk more — and in more depth — about their own life and career.

Listen closely to how Gross interviews her guests and note the effect these well-placed and highly informed references have. Listen for the doors they open and where her guests go once they walk through them.

As we've seen elsewhere, this isn't something that just happens. Gross has interviewed over 13,000 people. Yes, you read that right: 13,000 people! And she's assembled an exceptional team of researchers, producers, engineers, and show runners to provide an extraordinary level of breadth and depth to her interviews. That's another thing that sets Gross apart: She credits her team for all the work they put in to make *Fresh Air* the award-winning show it's been for the past 50 years.

How can you achieve the Terry Gross Effect?

Always be mindful of the fact that every conversation presents you with multiple opportunities to listen for the questions that will unlock the conversation the other person wants to have, even if they're not aware of the direction they want to go in. *Prepare* for conversations, don't just have them. And draw on your past conversations as if they were a reference library or a set of textbooks. Learn and apply what you've learned. Show up for the other person, whether they're your latest podcast guest or someone you've just met who's struck up a conversation while you're both waiting on line, without feeling the need to show off.

Larry King: Curiosity is the thing

You may have an opinion about the previous three interviewers I've mentioned, but I'll wager that none of them is as polarizing as Larry King. People either seem to love his approach or hate it — without much middle ground between the two. Regardless of where you stand, there's one thing that's undeniable: Larry King knew how to conduct an interview. After all, he'd done 50,000 of them over the course of his career.

In case you don't know about Larry King or aren't
familiar with his early career, he got his start on local
radio in Florida in the 1950s. He gradually rose
to national prominence hosting *The Larry King Show*,
a late-night interview and call-in program hosted
on the Mutual Broadcasting System. From there,
King went on to host *Larry King Live* on CNN from
1985-2010, which quickly became the highest-rated
talk show on TV.

Why was King so good?

This is another one of those ironies you've come
to expect from this book: King was such an excellent
interviewer because he led with curiosity, making
a habit, a very intentional habit, of under-preparing
for interviews so that nothing he did was rehearsed.

Talk about leaning into listening and trusting the moment!

But King was convinced that the best way to ask the
most engaging and revealing questions was to put
himself in the position of his listeners and viewers, who
were tuning in because they, too, were curious about his
guests — about who they were, what they aspired to,
and how they got to where they were.

King's audience didn't want a standard Q&A. They wanted the stories behind the Q&A. And that's what King delivered. When he interviewed someone, he became an empty vessel twice over, letting his guest and his audience steer the conversation.

Not that he'd become invisible. I mean, with those suspenders, he's hard to miss. But more than that, it was his enthusiasm that made his show irresistible during its run of over 6,000 episodes. King's unique, animated approach transformed him from being just another guy behind a desk asking questions into a sort of living prompt.

That's not to say King was simply winging it. He was far too skilled a listener for that. Instead, his process centered on being fully present in the moment. You know by now how hard that can be. Imagine doing it in front of thousands, tens of thousands, even millions of people! You wouldn't wing it either. You'd make sure you had a proven system in place (like the one you've been developing while reading this book), and you'd make sure you'd practiced it so often you could "get into the zone" whenever you needed to.

Like I said, it seems ironic, but King's "under-preparedness" was in fact a highly developed form of engaged listening. He'd avoid reading an author's latest book before interviewing them, for instance, not out of disrespect or a sense of superiority but because he wanted to stay curious about how and why the author had made the choices they had. It was his way of keeping things fresh.

I don't want to suggest any of these interviewers always got it right. King certainly didn't. After all, the guy conducted 50,000 interviews. He was bound to make mistakes. That said, imagine how refreshing his approach must have been, whether to first-time guests or people who'd been on the interview circuit for years if not decades.

Just think: After days, weeks, maybe even months of being asked the same questions over and over again, you're suddenly sitting across from someone who's asking you questions you haven't heard yet, questions that invite you to go beyond your latest project or that tabloid story you've been trying to distance yourself from. What a relief to be speaking with someone who's actually excited to hear about you — not the public persona, but the real you — someone who, unlike everyone else who's been interviewing you, has no preconceived notions of who the real you is.

I'd feel like sharing more, too. Wouldn't you?

Now imagine how transformative this can be in everyday conversation, which, as we've seen, tends to stay at the surface until the person you're talking to realizes you're really interested in what they have to say. Imagine showing up to every conversation you have with the same curiosity you had as a child, wanting to know so much more than just "I'm fine, thanks."

Except you don't need to imagine that — because you've been building that awareness and empathy and developing your own unique form of engaged listening this whole time.

Am I going to recommend you keep practicing listening every day, even once you've got your own system in place? You betcha. But I'm also going to encourage you to let your curiosity guide you more and more, even if that winds up leading you to an approach more in line with Terry Gross's than Larry King's. Because either way, you're going to be more dialed in to whomever you're speaking with, and they're going to see and sense that. And the trust you build by showing up and being fully present might just open an opportunity neither of you anticipated.

One of my favorite moments on *Larry King Live* was actually one of his more famous f@%*-ups. I think you'll see why immediately. Here's what happened: King was interviewing Jerry Seinfeld, and he was making it clear with his questions that he hadn't "done his homework." Seinfeld got upset and called him out on it, feeling that King was disrespecting him.

King's response?

He apologized. Can you believe it? On CNN, in front of his entire audience, he admitted his signature approach hadn't been right in this case.

Our takeaway? Even when you've become an expert listener, even once you've established a reputation for being an exceptional interviewer or conversationalist, you're never going to reach a point where you get it right every time — and you're never going to lose the need for that critical phrase: "I'm sorry."

Let's Practice

Who do you love? Here's an opportunity for you to build your own "heroes list" to share. And to really dive into how and why each of the interviewers on your list exemplifies engaged listening. Here are a few questions to get you started:

- Who are 2-3 of your favorite interviewers?

- Why are they your favorites?

- Who were they influenced by, and how did they weave those influences together to create their own signature style?

- What are the lessons about listening you've learned from watching and/or listening to them?

- What's your favorite interview they've done?

- How did they interact with the guest(s) during that interview?

- What strategies and techniques from this book can you spot in their approach?

Listening to engage

Now that you're starting the final chapter, I hope your own experience has shown you how powerful engaged listening can be. Before we get to our final story, I want to mention that it's an especially difficult one. You'll find yourself in the ICU with someone who's faced with making a decision about whether to keep her brother alive, even though he was brain-dead, or to let him die. If that's not something you're ready for, then please set the book down and continue to practice the exercises we've covered. Once you're ready, you'll encounter a situation that required every single aspect of listening we've explored — and an ending that shows you how much of an impact you can have when you go from just listening to engaged listening.

Story time

You'll remember that I interned for a large hospital system in Nebraska as soon as I graduated from college. At the time, my goal was to get my PhD in ethics and become a professor. I was advised that this sort of internship would launch my academic career.

It just so happened that it followed right on the heels of my marriage. Angela and I had an amazing first month in Omaha after our move from Michigan, both personally and professionally. I'd learned so much and met so many amazing people during my orientation at the hospital — including the nun I mentioned earlier who was in charge of running the entire network of area hospitals.

After completing orientation, I was given a pager. Yes, you read that right. A pager. That's how long ago we're talking about here!

As you may know, nothing ever seems to happen during normal business hours in the medical field. That meant my mentor — you remember Robert, right? — had the pager three days a week, while I had it for the other four. Outside of the trainings we did, the nature of our work meant that whenever the pager went off it was because someone was in really bad shape, as in they were on the verge of dying or were clinically dead already but were still breathing.

We'd get a call about once every two weeks. Whenever it happened, we'd drive to whichever hospital had paged us. Once we got there, we'd report directly to the ICU or NICU for a briefing. We'd sit down with the doctors and the attending nurses. We'd be given a copy of the patient's chart. Sometimes the chaplain would be there, too.

Our job at that point was to translate the jargonese
the doctors and nurses were using so we could communicate to patients' families and caregivers without any
confusion. That said, we knew even before we sat
down that the prognosis couldn't get any worse.
Most of the patients we were paged about had had
one of two things happen. They'd either been in a car
accident, or they'd been shot in the head — and they'd
often been the one to pull the trigger.

If the patient happened to be a child, it almost always
meant one thing: They were in the NICU, and they
weren't going to make it. I dearly wish I could say we
were never called in on cases involving children who'd
been the victims of gun violence. Or who had tried
to take their own lives. But I can't. Because we were.

Regardless of the cause, by the time we arrived, the
patient would have been connected to life support
that helped maintain minimal bodily functions.

The story I'm about to share involved an adult patient
who'd been in a car accident. This happened about nine
months into my internship. The pager went off while

my wife and I were out mountain biking. She heard the beep even before I did.

The phone number showed up on the pager's screen. I immediately knew which hospital I needed to get to. My shoulders sagged, and my expression changed completely. Angela looked at me and saw the toll all this was taking. Once again, she asked, "How much longer can you do this?"

From the start, I'd thought of this as a rite of passage in my career. I needed to finish my internship to make it to the next step. But my soul hurt. And if I had to point to one moment when I knew beyond a doubt that I wasn't cut out for a career in biomedical ethics, that would be it. Because you can't care for others if you're not able to care for yourself.

When I got to the hospital, I was told that the patient had broken his neck, shattering his C-2 vertebrae. At least that's what stood out to me on his chart, as his whole back was broken and his brain was swelling. He'd also fractured his skull. There was only brain stem activity at this point, no higher brain function. He wasn't hooked up to anything yet, though, because his heart was still beating and he was breathing.

But with the damage we saw from the MRI, he wasn't ever going to wake up again. No matter what you're thinking right now based on the movies you may have seen or the articles you may have read, the truth is that people don't recover from scenarios like this. The medical research is clear. He was brain-dead.

The hospital room I walked into was totally silent, unlike a lot of ICUs, which tend to be scenes of chaos, with people screaming and wailing and crying uncontrollably. On the bed was a middle-aged man. 46. Dark hair protruding from his head bandages, he was swaddled in white sheets, a single tube extending from his right arm to an IV. There was a blood oxygen meter on his left index finger. It beeped. And that was the only sound I remember.

Before I entered, I was told his sister was in the room. I walked in. As a member of the ethics team, I didn't wear any sort of medical clothing. I simply had a name badge on a lanyard around my neck. It read: Matthew Halloran, Ethics.

That was it. Except for the fact that the picture on my ID stood in stark contrast to the environment: bald head, full red lumberjack beard, and a ridiculous, beaming smile, much like on the cover of this book.

"Mary?" I asked.

She looked up.

The accident had happened a little over three hours prior. She'd been sitting in the room for about an hour by the time I arrived. The doctor and attending nurse had already been in, as had the organ donation people and the chaplain.

She wanted to talk to someone in Ethics.

"I'm Matt," I said. "I'm here to answer any questions you have and help you with what I know is an incredibly difficult decision."

"Hi," she replied in a low, quiet voice without making eye contact.

I remained standing because we were supposed to take family members to a separate room so they didn't have to look at the person they were going to have to make decisions about. The research was clear about that, too. We were also told to use the patient's first name. Mary's brother's name was Mark.

I signaled to the door. Mary looked up, nodded,
and got up to follow me to the consolation room.
It looked a lot like a living room. There were couches
and indirect lighting. The decor reflected a progressive
approach to hospital designs. Classical music played
softly in the background. The art on the walls was
as calming as the music. Everything worked together
to promote a sense of peace.

I gestured to one of the couches. Mary sat, and I took
a seat in a chair next to her. She'd glanced at me a few
times as we'd walked down the hall. But there was no
small talk. There wasn't supposed to be.

After she got settled, I waited for her to make
eye contact.

Once she did, I asked her a single question. It's one
of the most powerful questions we can ask, because
it signals we're completely invested in the answer:
"What are you thinking?"

In cases like this, the conversation almost always took
one of two turns: The family would either trust the

doctors or they wouldn't. There was almost never any middle ground. At least at the start.

Mary had chosen to trust the doctors, and it was clear that she was making peace with the situation. But she knew her family wouldn't. They were devout Roman Catholics, and she knew that they'd insist on preserving her brother's life in any way possible.

Mary had understood what the doctors had told her. She said she'd seen something like this on the TV show *ER*. "I know Mark has left this earth," she said. "At least it was quick. I can feel he's no longer with us. He was my older brother, you know."

Her pace was slow and deliberate. Her volume was consistent, and her cadence showed me she'd thought this through for the hour she'd spent by her brother's bedside.

"I looked up to him more than anyone else in the world. He was my hero. Now he's gone. I don't know who I'll look up to now." She slowed down during these last sentences. Her cadence got choppy because she was trying to hold back tears. "I understand that life is random and things like this happen. But I sure wish it wouldn't have happened to him."

She started to cry. Hard. Tears were streaming down her face, and her nose was running. Telling someone else what she was thinking had made everything undeniably real.

This is where it gets even harder if you're the listener. You want to comfort the other person, to tell them it'll be OK. You want to ease their pain. But intervening, even if only to hand them a tissue, sends the wrong message: That you're uncomfortable and want them to stop. Let the person experience their emotions. Don't try to control the situation.

In this case, I simply waited for Mary to signal she was ready to continue the conversation, just as Robert and I had been trained to do. If there's one thing you take away from this chapter, please let it be this: Don't try to hasten someone's grief. Sit with them. Listen. Let them cry. Let them be the one to tell you when they're ready for your help. Otherwise, you're likely to do more harm than good.

A few minutes later, Mary said: "I'm my brother's medical power of attorney. I know his wishes. I know he'd want me to let him go, give every organ to anyone that could use it. He always told me that if he could save anyone with his death, he wanted to. He was an amazing person."

Instead of responding immediately, I took a deep breath, maintaining eye contact. I softened my gaze even more. I nodded without saying anything, using the 5-second rule before I even knew I was using it. "The issue is my family is going to fight this," Mary continued. "I told the hospital that they'd threaten to sue even though I have power of attorney and have been legally appointed to make medical decisions for my brother — the decisions he actually wrote down and wanted."

Her voice started to get louder, faster, and more staccato. I could hear the anger starting to creep in.

Even though biomedical ethicists are trained in the multiple stages of grief, I always marveled at how quickly some people move through the range of emotions when someone they know and love is dying or has died.

Mary's face turned red. Her fists clenched. Her face tightened. "What do I do?" she asked.

This wasn't a question I could answer, personally or professionally. Mark wasn't my brother, and I was ethically bound not to do anything other than provide Mary with support as she made the decision about her brother's care.

I waited. The longer I could be silent, the greater the chance she would realize the decision was entirely hers to make.

While I sat quietly, she suddenly turned her anger on me, yelling, "What good are you? Aren't you the ethics guy? Aren't you supposed to say something?"

I took another slow breath, making sure she saw that I wasn't sighing or being dismissive in any way.

"Yes, I'm allowed to talk," I replied, my volume a little lower than usual. My pace was also slow and deliberate: "But I'm here to support you in making your decision, which, you're totally right, is legally yours to make. I can't possibly answer for you or your brother. Nor would I ever presume to do so, even if I wish I could make this easier for you. Decisions like this are never easy, and I'm sorry your family won't be supportive."

Her face softened. Her fists unclenched. She stood up and walked over to me. I was still sitting at this point. She reached out her hand. I took it. She gently pulled me out of my chair. And then she hugged me, holding on as tightly as she could.

I gently hugged her back.

Her body started to shudder. I felt tears wetting my shirt. I didn't move or make a sound. I just held her.

I don't know how much time passed. After a while, she stopped crying, although she didn't let go of me.

Then she did. Slowly, she backed away. At first, she wouldn't make eye contact. It was like she was ashamed for what she'd just done. She walked back over to the couch I'd led her to when we'd first entered the room. As she sat down, she looked at me again.

"You're the first person to really listen to me."

I smiled gently.

"Ever," she said. "Thank you. I know what I need to do now." She bowed her head, just a little, and then she pushed herself to her feet.

It was extremely hard for me to write my report the next day. I really didn't know what to say. But what I did know, and what I hope is evident after reading this chapter and the book as a whole, is that what we often need isn't someone else's advice but their attention, not their words but their willingness to listen, and to truly hear what we have to say, especially when we're not entirely sure what that is until we've said it.

What I knew then and still know now is that Mary made the right decision. That's true because she made it after having had the chance to reflect on what she and her brother had decided. No one else stepped in to advise her. No one else pressured her or questioned her right to make the decision. Mary had taken the time to walk herself through her thoughts and feelings, and she'd been comforted knowing she'd had someone quietly in her corner supporting her as she did.

Imagine having that same reassurance when you're faced with your next difficult decision. Or being the person someone else entrusts to listen as they wrestle with an impossible decision of their own.

It may be that those conversations, as one-sided as they can seem, are the most important and impactful in our lives, because they allow us to see ourselves and others at our strongest and most vulnerable, our most decisive and least assured. And they remind us that there'll come a time in each of our lives when what we need more than anything isn't the courage of someone else's conviction but the permission to listen to our own voice rising toward clarity.

Let's Practice

As you continue to engage people in conversation, you'll be faced with situations like the one in this chapter. Marshal all your engaged listening skills so you can hold space for the other person so they can find their own answers to the life-changing questions they've been confronted with. Give them every reassurance you're listening and hearing everything they're saying — but empower them with the knowledge and awareness that they hold the keys to their own future, however challenging that future may be. Lend them kindness and support, but also make it clear that you're an empty vessel they can fill until the resolution and reassurance they're looking for is suddenly in focus. Show them how impactful it can be when someone else is truly seen and heard. And give them the chance to start practicing engaged listening so they can go out and change the world for the better, too.

Outro

This is where you'd usually expect to hear congratulations, right? I mean, you've just finished reading an entire book and doing a series of intensive exercises in order to become a better listener.

So, before we go any further, I want to say it so you and everyone you know can hear it: CONGRATULATIONS! Having put in all this time and effort, you're well on your way to becoming an engaged listener.

At the same time, you know by now that being an engaged listener isn't something you graduate into. It's not a peak to summit. It's a daily practice. Which means you need to keep doing it to stay fluent.

I know the thought of endless practice can seem unappealing, especially when you're itching to get into the game. But, just like those pro basketball players we met earlier, you've already started to reap the rewards of that level of dedication, so I know you're putting this book down having built the habits that will allow you to continue to excel as a listener and learner.

Not only that, but I'm confident you'll continue

to open doors for other people to become engaged listeners, too, because you know firsthand how much we all stand to gain by having more people actually listening whenever they're in the room.

OK, before we both sign off for now (until you pick up the book again or reach out to connect), let's take a look at a few of the main points we've covered:

1. Engaged listening means going from listening as a way to bide time to listening with your full attention so that everything you say starts with first having heard others.

2. There are different types of communicators. Identify them quickly and your relationships will flourish.

3. The greatest and most rewarding journey in life is to learn about yourself. Learn everywhere, all the time.

4. Giving someone the space to be heard is one of the most powerful and generous things you can do.

5. You earn trust whenever you show someone you're truly listening to them.

6. There's no better way to convince someone to make changes in their life than to show them you've heard what they've said.

7. Leadership starts with listening, learning, and asking questions.

8. Whenever you're not sure what to do, just shut the f@%# up and listen. You'll be amazed at how often you find just what you'd been looking for.

Having come all this way together, I want to thank you from the bottom of my heart for spending so much time with me. I hope these stories, anecdotes, and exercises have helped you feel more confident and comfortable when you're not talking — as well as when you are.

The world needs people like you who are dedicated to listening — truly listening — because so many people feel alone and unheard. Every time you hold space for someone who feels ignored, under-appreciated, or misunderstood, you change the world for the better.

And the more often that happens, the better off we all are!

With love and gratitude,
Matt

Acknowledgments

I'll always be grateful to Angela Halloran, who has from the start been my person. As you've seen, she was around for most of these stories, and she's stuck with me through them all. When we met, I wasn't an engaged listener yet. She's taught me more about life and listening than I could ever acknowledge.

I want to thank Derek Pollard at Constellar Creative for his patience and expertise in helping me develop what was a loose collection of stories into the book you've just read or listened to. He provided invaluable insights and feedback throughout the writing and editing process — and became a practiced hand at the 5-second rule you'll learn about.

Thanks, too, to Anne and Chafe Hensley at Weirder Wonderland. They say you can't judge a book by its cover. I'm convinced Anne and Chafe have proved that theory wrong once and for all! Their creativity and design savvy are amazing, and they're an absolute pleasure to work with. Thank you both.

Additionally, I'd like to thank Kirk Lowe, my longtime business partner; George Kinder; Dr. Victor Harms;

Chris Kirkpatrick; the station crews at WIDR FM and WKDS FM; Bob Badra; the members of Radiohead and Sigur Rós, along with anyone who's ever played baroque music; Jim Henson; and every single person who supports The Muppets.

About the author

Meet Matt Halloran, a storyteller, speaker, and advocate for genuine connection in a world filled with noise. With a heart fueled by empathy and a mind honed by over two decades of experience, Matt has made it his mission to bridge the gap between people through the transformative power of listening.

In his compelling book, *Shut the F Up and Listen*, Matt shares raw, real-life stories and practical insights that cut through the chaos of modern life. He understands the deep longing for connection and offers a roadmap for those seeking to understand and be understood.

Drawing from his journey of overcoming communication barriers, Matt's words resonate with authenticity and compassion. His message is simple yet profound: the most powerful act is to listen in a world where everyone wants to be heard.

Matt brings his stories to life as a captivating speaker, igniting hearts and sparking conversations that matter. He invites audiences to join him on a journey of empathy and understanding, where every word spoken and listened to has the potential to change lives.

Matt Halloran is more than just an author; he's a guide, a friend, and a beacon of hope for those yearning to connect in a disconnected world. For a glimpse into his world of heartfelt communication, visit Matt's website at matthalloran.com.

www.ingramcontent.com/pod-product-compliance
Lightning Source LLC
Chambersburg PA
CBHW020251130626
46549CB00005B/2170